NUGGETS FROM

A QUEEN

A 365 DAY DEVOTIONAL

WRITTEN BY

QUEEN OYA

ISBN 979-8-88992-432-6

Cover Design by Leeds Graphics.
Editorial by Leeds Press Corp
Written by Ginny Atkinson

Leedspublishing.com
Twitter.com/ Leedspresscorp
Instagram.com/ Leedspresscorp
Facebook.com/ Leedspresscorp
LP BOOKS is an imprint of LEEDS PRESS CORP. Name and Logo is a trademark of LEEDS PRESS CORP. The publisher is not responsible for websites (or their content) that are not owned by the publisher.
LEEDS PRESS SPEAKERS AGENCY provides a wide range of authors for speaking events.
To find out more; info@leedspress.com or call 323-230-0062
Printed in the United States of America.

CONTENTS

DAY 1

Today can begin the first day of a new attitude of gratitude! Whatever we believe for is surely possible for us, as we change our attitudes; we change the words we speak. This is the perfect time to change our words, minds, lifestyle and beliefs. We see Faith work when we can be privileged to peep into our future and see our lives prosper. Today see yourself moving forward and up into the promise of healing, prosperity, a spiritual growth. All these things bring us closer to Faith, which connects to our God who can do all things.

See yourself in your dream home, owning your own company, taking care of others, fulfilling the vision, driving that luxury vehicle, walking around ditches instead of in them, living above, leading and lending, laughing in pure joy, loving the unlovable, breaking curses, restoring your finances with increase, filling your every need. Today, as we speak it, we must BELIEVE it and Faith will work so we can receive it. Happy— not sad or depressed, New—nothing old or used, Year— not minutes or days but year. All this Year, stay new and happy!

DAY 2

What's the password? Anything you value must be secure—your diamonds, pearls, bonds, important documents, treasure etc. aren't displayed for anyone to take or destroy. We secure valuables, if we are wise, we lock our doors, gates, cars, and even our electronics for security. Why? We want protection. We need assurance so we many times get insurance for assurance, (laugh out loud).

What's the password to your assurance, protection, security etc.? How many times can't you remember your password,

need to reset it, had it hacked or needed to create another one? Whether it's a password, lock, or code—are we secure? Is it trusted? Who protects your security that you've secured, who hides your password, who mastered your keys? We don't know, but when our trust is in God within, we're fully secured, protected, and possess the keys to the Kingdom.

DAY 3

Success and the word NO being used in the same sentence seems unreal. Do you know how to find out if it's really love??? Tell them NO!! If they still embrace you and find no reason to leave, they should be a keeper. A real salesperson cannot allow the word NO to stop, discourage or define their success.

NO, equips us for a YES. Every NO gets us closer to a YES. It's not rejection, it; a delay. To succeed in life, we must know that NO is the right step, possible at the wrong time. Or it could prepare you to also chime this word more frequently so you can remain on course. No, I don't need to be liked by you to love me. NO, I choose to be different and if it's not popular I'm more than okay. NO, I don't have the money to spare for you. NO, I won't give up on my dream, children, life, vision, lifestyle, personality, relationships or Faith. I choose to be successful, faithful, lovable, accountable, teachable, rooted, truthful, decisive, reachable and stable. Say NO to some dream killers, haters, backstabbers, users and abusers (weeds in our garden) and see Success more clearly and defined. NO!

DAY 4

Nuggets...What is a nugget? It's a small lump of gold or other precious metal found ready-formed in the earth. It can

be a nugget of gold; a valuable idea or fact—Nuggets of Information. As we were given Nuggets from Heaven, valuable forms of wisdom are fully poured from our heaven. We all are nuggets from heaven—valuable pieces that are sometimes broken, sometimes overlooked, many times sought after, oftentimes desired and yet very seldom appraised. What's the going rate of what you possess? We are Kings and Queens, living in a Kingdom that has been given to us with many nuggets. Today begins our journey to doors we might have overlooked.

DAY 5

Declare it to the world today—because this is a good day that ends the old and begins the new. Had some disappointments, sickness, losses, setbacks, discouragements, enemies, and hurt but you made it? You overcame areas you thought wasn't attainable, saw some things that seem impossible, met some people who were unforgettable, done some things others marked as incredible and lived a life that you felt was impossible. To all that, I would say, "I made it." Got a few scars to remind you of the pain, but I made it. Lost some haters in the game, but I made it. Doctors called it, medicine couldn't cure it, but I made it. Didn't get to do all I had dreamed, but I made it. Bank account never seems to measure up to what I had on my list, but I made it. Things turned out better than what I began and somehow—I made it. So let them talk, point, lie and shout out the bad and ugly because I got good news, I MADE IT!

DAY 6

Consequences... we all will have them; bitter or sweet, love or hate, together or apart, today or tomorrow. We've heard it said "Be careful with the dishes you spoon out, you may have to eat it." We're allowed to make our own choices and with them, we can absorb our consequences. Some say, "Karma is best served hot with friends and cold with enemies." Everything is spinning quickly, food served fast, relationships ending promptly, money dwindling rapidly, cars meant for speeding, words flowing abruptly and life ending daily. There's a time we must slow down emotions, spending, driving, eating, careless living and working so we can enjoy our lives and our purpose for being. There will be decisions to make, words to honor, people to forgive, hearts to be mended, lives to change and consequences for them all. So carefully listen before serving that dish, it may taste better served than eaten. I'm just saying…

DAY 7

I am declaring this to every believer today, despite any obstacles, changes, controversies, lies, habits, relationships or battles; we will win and shall live. The enemy knows that the clock is running out and must distract, mislead, hinder, confuse, fight, manipulate, bring fear, stress, doubt and try to destroy every, promise, plan and purpose. We decree that we've been given the abundant life, prosperity, power to overcome, cast down, bind and deliver those in captivity. No matter what comes your way from day to day, we shall LIVE! We are under mighty protection. Suicide, murder, sickness, stress, accidents, drugs, alcohol, AIDS can't take us away from the plans and our future. Live!!!

DAY 8

Ever wonder why you are given time to regroup, rethink or resign? There are times when you have to reevaluate your position—are you winning or losing? Sometimes you're knocked in a corner, taking blow after blow and falling, failing and losing is the outcome if you don't regroup, rethink or resign. Find what was not working and search for a plan to win. Are you in shape to go in as you are, or do you need to regroup, rethink or resign? Half time is in place to take the players away from the battleground so they can get another look at the win ahead. They place a windshield in front of you, so you are looking through the rearview mirror of what's behind you. They may look like they are winning— you may have taken some hard hits; but get back to you corner; cuz you're covered. You can't lose if we're listening to words of wisdom, so let's get ready to rumble. We got this; we can't fail or lose when we've listened to what we've been instructed to do.

DAY 9

Amazingly, before there were medicines, there were our grandmothers or great grandmothers who use to give us some king of herb. It worked. When children would cut up in school, there was no resource officer, our parents resources hung in a tree. When our parents didn't agree, they didn't separate to different beds, they snored it away. No need calling a marriage counselor, they knew who did it. They talked about it or yelled about it and still stuck to their marriage vows. Yes, I remember when Castor oil was the only medicine we had besides the limb from the tree—it worked. What are you fond memories that you wish you could have today?

DAY 10

Sometimes we just need to clear our minds, detox our lives and make better decisions. What we do know is, most of where we are, who we are and what we possess has been from the choices we've made.

When we're desperate, confused, hurt, angry or an emotional wreck; we can make some of the worse moves. Like to be upset and go excessive shopping, buying stuff we don't need with the funds we know are destined for other things. We could choose the wrong partner, location, words or project, when we're not focused.

That's why we must find time to meditate, which we're supposed to do throughout the day. This is where we can detox ourselves from unhealthy thoughts, people, foods, habits and decisions. Let's take time to silence everything around us and listen within; we may be surprised to what we may hear. Sometimes I ride in my car, sit in my room or outside in silence, to listen to spiritual insights.

DAY 11

Are we landing without clearance? Let's mount up on wings as eagles, mount up and soar. Soar until we're led to land. Sounds simple? Then why do we find that we've got power to soar and then we hear (hear) of a storm, find arrows trying to kill us and become tired? When we get tired, we then look for a place to land. But have you been cleared for landing. If not—then we are landing (finding places to stop into, at or by) without clearance. Make sure that we're hearing correctly, when you have power to soar, make sure you got clearance to land. If not—we could be landing in the middle of the enemy's trap, arena, plot, schemes, and or death. Wake-

up, make-up, get up, stand up, show up, power up and look up. To soar is a gift and to land is to empower this gift to others. I receive, believe and shall achieve.

DAY 12

When you know you're walking on water! When you're able to do things that seems impossible to others. Can you touch a dream, see the future, stand on mountains and travel to limitless places? Then and only then can you become limitless, fearless, endless and fabulous.

Life is what we choose to make it, how we choose to see and most definitely who we decide to include in it. Carry the torch and go places others dreamed of being at and seeing. It's one thing to be seen, it's another to see but you've arrived when you can do both without missing a beat.

DAY 13

Early this morning as I was meditating, this was shared with me. So many times, in our lives, we find later how immature our ways have been. Every day is a great day to rise up and make it work in our favor. Yesterday is gone, along with its joy or pain but today we can make it better.

We can correct all mistakes; heal from heartaches and administer life within. So, be absolutely great at being your best you and take no negativity in your space. We're winners prepared for life's battles. Be the peace in a storm, the sugar in the honeycomb and the wind beneath the wings (felt that one).

DAY 14

A cake isn't a cake until it's been baked. Wondering why you are battling that spirit over and over? Glad you askedJ. Look at the years of that struggle, the price you have paid, the hours lost, the people you have lost, found, hurt, disappointed, confused and the chaos you have endured. Now check your cake, your life, your injuries, your mind, your faith and your love. This wasn't to destroy you; it's to bake your cake. It took the flour to mix with the eggs, oh yes, mixing isn't as easy as it seems. Your life is tossed around until you can see you withstood the mix. Then the oil is poured in (the anointing) to bring you to the top of that hell, storm, lie, relationship, promotion, health issues and mental state. Now the oven experience is your test, and this world isn't to destroy you, but to bring you to (A baked cake). Bake well because the outcome is awesome.

DAY 15

Sometimes we are at sea and our boat (our lives) seem so unsteady, hopeless and defeated because of the beatings of the storms, the weight of the loads it must bear, the winds that blows to capsize or throw you off course and the hungry sharks that await your fall. As you look at the doom, the last call and the final strike, there's a light from afar. You're not far from your answer, your deliverance, your moment of truth, your promise, the new life, breakthrough, healing, the sounds of victory, your door, your instructions, your home, car, child, flight, peace, love, and etc. This storm is to inform your hater, takers, foes, family and pretenders that you got a seed in you, a destiny, a nation, ministry, a forest, a legacy, a multitude following, work to complete, lives to change and mountains

to soar. I needed this storm to break some habits, lose some vampires and confuse the enemy. I found my second chance, wind, opportunity and life. I need to take another look at the chains, lies, beatings and weapons that tried to block me, from another view! Somebody needs to declare your future into the atmosphere and go into your purpose. Can you see your light?

DAY 16

Ever notice how the enemy cheers you when you're on his team, doing his bidding and his slave? But when you decree and declare a change of heart, mind, body and soul, he wages war and puts out a bounty for your life. Look back at those that were in bondage and hell with you and notice they too aren't cheering your release and freedom. You haven't lost family, friends or foes; you've gained back your rites. I'm an angel having some earthly experiences, what about you? If you find your circle becoming smaller, you're doing something right. Can somebody check the climate, feels like another Boom in position? Grab your shades; the light is shining on you. So do a wing check and prepare for takeoffs. Oh, I feel it flowing out of my belly, another chance to take the stand for you and you! You're free, you're powerful! You made it! You're clear for takeoff. Boom!

DAY 17

My soul seeks to be fed and hungers after some finger turning pages of my mind. Eagerly to satisfy this craving, I find myself meditating on the word; grace. Where would we be this day, if grace wasn't on our menu? Grace is undeserving

favor, Selah. Grace stopped the severity of the punishment I should've gotten with just, "you're forgiven." You know death should've been our demise (end) but grace...You know the curtains could've been pulled back and shown the world our nakedness shame, sin, failures, lies and shortcomings but ... Yes, imagine our lives without grace and then ask yourself exactly who, what and how if it hadn't been for grace following you all day. Whoa, my SOUL is being filled with the food from above; we'll call it "Nuggets from Heaven". Soul Food—my favorite delicacy; slowly savored, mixed with a lot of love and carefully chosen to make you go mmm, mmm good. Love yah!

DAY 18

Good morning, it's another Triumphant Tueday! Every problem isn't our problem. Some problems are problems needing solutions; we're not always the solution. When we think of problems, we see a matter that looks uncomfortable, can be stressful and will feel unreasonable. Know this, every problem has an anger; some are easy, some available, some doable, others uncomfortable and not agreeable but still the answer; nevertheless. Instead of focusing on our or any problem, let's be more directed to the solution.

It's not a problem until we make it one. Adjusting, rethinking, organizing, preparing and maintaining are valuable keys to any problem. Get ready to attack, challenge, laugh, move or reexamine the problem, then go to faze two. Positive flows bring great powerful energy.

DAY 19

Desperate /Desperado is defined as a person with no hope; A person that was not stopped; law breaker. The song says "why don't you come to your senses?" Desperate means, very serious or dangerous having an urgent need, desire, someone who wants something so bad that they will go to extreme lengths to get it.

Sometimes we just have to sit back and relax because the world is on stage. Become a quieter student and observe every teacher. Every lesson: good, bad and ugly should teach us something, it's hard to learn when we're not paying attention.

The wrong people can teach us the right things; I've learned to tell those who've worked hard to destroy or block my future; "thank you". Because I know if that wasn't done, I couldn't have learned the bigger lesson. You would rather lose a hundred dollars at this level than a thousand at the next. Thank those desperados becuz their lessons will promote you, if you pay attention. Know that EVERYONE IS A TEACHER! So, what would it take to make you desperate or a desperado?

DAY 20

Put the Word on it, every trial and test that comes is to try the word you have in you. Healing comes through the words we speak. The word is too big for our micro problems when we know how to use it. When our problems are consuming us and seem as a mountain, then our word has gotten too small. We all go through our storms, big or small, but always remember; we can speak to our storms and tell it to "shut up", the only way you can be powerful is when you're using the word, studying so you can win your test and trials. Many people are falling away from the truth. Don't be one of them. The Word

is your weapon, so put "The Word in it and live the abundant life."

DAY 21

Checking the reservations! How many times you thought you had booked a reservation and believed you were in, only to find out, there's a problem? Making plans to be in a place, with someone or doing something at a specific time and Boom! You can't get to the destination you planned. You can't have the person you desire and you're unable to do what you had hoped. In all this chaos, you become lost in the shuffle; you are torn with decisions, fighting with yourself and unable to pray. Then, it hits you! Where are my reservations? Am I supposed to be here? Did I arrive on schedule? Have I paid the full price? Ahh, the price!

My payment, I didn't lay aside every weight and energy, I couldn't forgive those who hurt me, bruised me, betrayed me and walked away. I made some messes I haven't cleaned up. I need to empty my hurts, relieve my stress, make deposits of pure love and gather my spiritual heart. Reservations check anybody?

DAY 22

Have you ever slept with the enemy? If so, why? We can be in the company of someone we've believed to be a partner, friend or confidant to later find out; it was an enemy. Many of us are sleeping, spending idle time with or snuggling up to those who have no desire to see us win.

Not everyone that desires to be close to us, wants to uplift, push or empower, some only need to be close enough to drain,

set up, discover our weakness or destroy us. So, be careful of those that we choose to sleep, whisper, confide, release or befriend. Are they a friend or foe?

DAY 23

What's that smell? No, not the turkey and all the fixings—but that stank? What's stinking in your life? Have we heard a word yet? We can't hurry the process! There are many times we're asked to handle a situation, close some doors or let go of some people but we linger with it until it begins to stink.

When the problem gets so bad and the smell is unbearable, we must deal with it, find out what and where, and then eliminate it. It doesn't matter; we must come out of it before we're consumed by the stink. Whatever the mess we're in or the purpose for the mess, we possess the power to move it.

Now, what's that smell? Is it VICTORY over death, hell and the grave? You've been loosed; it's your choice to be FREE!

DAY 24

Most people have trained themselves to say the right things while doing the wrong thing. It takes an exceptional mind to always listen to what they're not saying. It's the hidden things that could cause us pain, loss, misunderstanding and brokenness.

Be firm at being truthful even if it's not pleasant or acceptable. When we speak and live honestly; our mouths, hearts and spirits are all aligned and speaking the same things. Listen…

DAY 25

We're guaranteed promises; that if our tree is good or bad, so will be our fruit. How many times have we missed the root of a thing because we were watching the problem not the cause? We are a tree connected to deep roots that has expanded over years and miles and yet remain strong. Imagine all that the tree has endured through storms, fires, floods and horrific acts of evil.

Our tree of whatever species is designed to cover, provide, support, and bring comfort and life but never to deny itself its purpose. How many of us have denied our purpose because we didn't know it or couldn't fulfill it? It is a freak of nature for an orange tree to bring forth pecans or a pineapple tree to produce olives. Be mindful that whatever we're called to do or be, we must perform because to be anything different isn't going to be profitable.

We are having different purposes with our tree of life but still we are all called to give life and produce. Let's check our fruit!

DAY 26

Alcohol, drugs, death, influences, curses, trouble, sex-addicts! This morning we want to think about the many addictions in our lives. Some we've practiced, some we've inherited, some we've skilled. Studies have stated that it takes 21 days to create a habit. Hmm! So if you do anything for 21 days in a row—you will build a habit, start a cycle, become an addict. 21 days, 3 weeks, 7 is the number of completion—so 3 x 7—everybody say "COMPLETE". If you start a bad habit, a cursed thing, a death wish or strong cycle in the negative, imagine TURNING IT AROUND. Let's build a new us. Let's build better character, strong relationships, better financial choices, words of wisdom, awesome attitudes, Meditation, soul searching and positive loving. 21 days, are you ready for an addiction that will change your life anew?

DAY 27

How many times have someone tried to sell us a dream? When our lives are in desperate need of a right now fixed; here comes the dreamer or schemer. If we're not careful, we'll buy into the lie, hoping that it'll be true; let's not be an easy prey.

Never show a heart broken, a mind confused or a life unsuccessful; it's a sure magnet for a predator. Don't be a prey.

DAY 28

Find your place of serenity and stay there. There will always be something, someone or some place that will challenge our place of peace, just remain in park.

No one can fully know the journey we've been on, the hits we've taken or the victories we've won. Stop trying to explain to a people who are truly not interested in our wins but just our defeats. We're not here by chance, we're here by assignment. Speak life, success, peace and love into the atmosphere and our universe will bring it to us. Let's keep on living our best life, against all odds.

DAY 29

All day we're given choices; to do right or wrong, lie or tell the truth, obey or disobey, pray or be silent, give up or go forward, make friends or be friendless, step out on faith or

remain in fear, build or destroy, stand or fall, be at peace or torment, follow life or death, pay or owe!

When we make our choice, we must also abide by the results of that decision; good, bad or indifferent. As we look over our lives, we must understand that where we are today is 90% of a choice we made in our yesterday(s). If we're not where we want or desire to be, let's make better choices on today.

DAY 30

Are you able to see? Can you spot the Judas in your life? Look how he stayed so close to his master; he knew his every move and even mingle with the others— to the point that no one recognized him to be different. He was given no special treatment and was accepted into the fold with love.

You can love your enemies but don't allow them to betray you with a kiss or trust. Our love will lift us up above all the Judas's in our lives. Everybody smiling isn't smiling for and with you. They may be out to get you. Be careful of those in your circle. There may be a need to change your circle or cover your cheeks. Can you see clearly now?

DAY 31

Are we in a Relationship? Relationships aren't supposed to be centered on looking at the outside. It is sometimes centered on how to look the part, act the part, and talk the part— but denying the part of a heart-relationship. Relationships are to be intimate. It is passionate, caring, loving, always desiring to be in the close company of, seeks to please privately, goes beyond to ensure security and trust, protects, fulfills, impacts so no other can find you empty. Love sacrifices all and values

truth. How do you know how strong your boat, life, family, marriage, resources and faith is without the test of a storm?

DAY 32

How many times have you said something or done something and waited for the connection? Have you ever been on your phone and was talking for a while and realize there was no one on the other end? It's moments like this that we understand that we may be talking to someone but there's no connection.

A connection is when we're able to have a strong signal of reception and deliverance. When we've connected to familiar spirits; there's an immediate jolt or celebration because it doesn't happen often. Many times in seeking for connection; we become frustrated and lose hope. Remember everything is connected to something; we just need to know where we're connected to.

Note this: if the connection is wrong; disconnect immediately.

DAY 33

Acceptance. Most of us are always seeking to be accepted by someone, some place or something. Once we have learned to accept ourselves, the work becomes easier. We draw our own lines of what's acceptable to and in our lives. When we learn to hear our own music inside, we'll dance for the world to see.

Too many of us have orchestrated our lives within everyone else's confinement and have no idea who we are. Freedom always begins inside and once we've accepted ours, it's beauti-

ful. You can't be me nor I be you; we all got our own uniqueness that we must accept and define.

DAY 34

You never realize how tough life is until you try living it right. The day you try living right, is the day our enemy within us starts attacking who we are. All those years of drinking, fighting and anything else we're doing—it seems you have no problem until the day you say I want to get my life together. That is the day we have to have the whole armor on because it's not an easy task fighting ourselves—keep your eye on the goal and stay focused. You can handle the rest. Through trials and tribulations, storms of life and through the hell you will go through— you'll find out how strong you really are. Keep your eyes on the prize.

DAY 35

Let's live a lifestyle that makes anyone wonder what we are doing that they aren't. Sometimes in our worse places and our most devastated moments, we still like a hero to someone else. So, keep on rising to the top, be like the oil we are designed to be because it never loses the power to rise.

Some may call it the Hustle, but you must know it to be just a Flow. Be great and don't stop.

DAY 36

Everyone doesn't hear, see or think the same and that's understandable. One baby may crawl at nine months; another is walking while another can read. These different levels have a lot to do with the surrounding environment. What we're introduced to become our way of thinking, moving and developing. Be inquisitive, go beyond the break, seek deep truths, refuse to give up and build success stories.

Be the person that will be missed when gone because your presence is so rewarding. Be exceptional and a forever memory; when someone says, "I miss or missed you", make sure they mean it.

DAY 37

The world is our oyster as we search for the pearl. Some call it a quest, some a journey yet we should all agree that it's a search. What are we searching for? Whatever it is, our universe possesses it, no matter how big or small. Our teens are hit with identity crisis; trying to figure out who and what they're destined to be.

Our identity is so multifaceted, some many layers, levels and brilliance that it's hard to balance at times. Know that every search will bring us closer to sweet truths and priceless information. Remember this, we're all on our own personal journey seeking what will fulfill us, when we find it; hold it dear and don't let it go.

DAY 38

Make sure your reservoir is large enough to hold what's coming back. Because everything we sent out must come back and usually it's multiplied. So, whatever we're receiving is mostly coming from our giving out. All the great things we've done; people we've fed or clothed every kind word and every positive thing must be returned. Things are produced because no seed in fertile ground can lie still, it must come forth.

Just as any and all negative energy will overflow. So, choose your source, then be ready for the comeback and don't question the Universe; just check our spiritual motives.

DAY 39

Everyday we're given the chance to make a moment. Whether we choose to make someone laugh, cry, want to be with us or walk away from us; it's our moment.

Most people want to laugh becuz laughter is a great medicine; it takes away some problems, stress and can bring us to another level. Yet, sometimes it's time to think about a serious moment that will cause us to reflect.

As I was growing up, I saw some bad things, I had to make a decision to take this experience and make it better me not bitter me. Today is our day to laugh or cry, be better or bitter, happy or say; what are we going to do? Think about it!

DAY 40

"Who is going to move this stone away? Instead of looking around, let's move it because it'll bring us close to the answer, breakthrough, truth, miracle and etc. Then we'll be able to rise up to receive, claim and enjoy all that we've been afraid to pursue.

We'll get the strength, will power, understanding, Faith or knowledge to move the stone. So don't worry about the stone that should or could have hindered your victory. Every stone, disease, hindrance, lie, curse, struggle, demon, forgotten word, promise, purpose, soul, testimony, child, wife, husband, disagreement, prison, hospital, grave—has to move! Who's going to move the stone? What Stone?

DAY 41

Trust! Trust is a very difficult thing to do when there's been no testing yet! Who do we trust? Do we truly know that everything is being shaped, covered, changed, arranged, anointed, and released into the atmosphere? Do you believe in our greatest security system? We must believe that we are never alone, and nothing comes our way without guidance and purpose.

If, we're facing it, then we got the skills and power to win it, learn from it and grow in it. The very things that seem to take us down today will always elevate us later. Trust the process, even if and when you don't trust yourself or others.

DAY 42

Can we say Turn it around? Yes, this is the day we want a turnaround to be manifested. Every one of us can ask ourselves while on our merry-go-round, where's the gain, has this cycle ended, when will this thing stop and will I survive the ride? The cycle of sickness, broken hearts and relationship, spiritual battles, emptiness, emotional wars, poverty, ignorance, dissatisfaction, insecurity, lies and betrayals, to name a few. Coming out of the craziness is only the first step, and then your heart and mind must be fixed on keeping free which takes WORK. Around and around we go—test after test, battle after battle, struggle after struggle and crash after crash. Eyes swollen from tears, body tired, heartbroken, life decaying, spirit starving, knees bruised, friends vanishing and yet it turns around in our favor!

DAY 43

Are you afraid to go forward, because you've stumbled so many times in your past? Afraid to step into a miracle due to the mess you're wrestling with today? Are you afraid to believe in promises when you struggle to keep yours? Afraid to live in the overflow when you've lost so much in the just enough? Well, sometimes you've got to forget everything you think you know and lean in. Listen to the heartbeat. Does it skip a beat? Speed up and race or remain the same? Our spirit isn't nervous, perplexed, frighten, unsure or weak? When you're unsure of the promises, your place, their desire, his heart, her state of mind, or the next move –than just rest on the words—He's got next. You'll always have the power to praise, power to believe on what has already been done, power to know what has begun in us can rest in us. Just "be still and know that I am

God." Who or what causes you to forget your power?

DAY 44

Who or what are we ashamed of? What are we called into that we run from? Have you ever been ashamed to confess you love for someone, stand with someone or speak up against a wrong? How can we love someone and be ashamed of them at the same time or can we?

How can we love and stand with someone behind close doors and publicly deny them access to our world? Whether it's our financial state, martial state, mental state, physical or spiritual state; we must be ready to declare in anyone's presence. Whatever state we're in is only temporary, so don't be ashamed of it, claim it and then re-define it into a greater place. Wherever we are today is purposed to make, shake and awake us so never be ashamed of being used to becoming greater.

DAY 45

We all have been carefully given us the ability to gain based on our willingness to WORK! Yes, Work! You can't grow or mature if you're not reading, studying, or listening. When you've got idle time, are we studying what's happening in this world? Or are we following: candy crush, face book, television, texting, Instagram, meaningless conversations and lifestyles. You can't give what you don't have. No more excuses. What are you doing with what you got? Fair warning!

Sometimes you've got to walk away from that which is lost and has no desire to be found and focus on the task at hand. Get tired of them, not Him! Sounds like it's time for a change, so let's get ready.

DAY 46

The splendor of the butterfly! The lowly caterpillar lives only to become a butterfly, (purpose). On its journey, it eats milky leaves only; any other insect or animal that eats that plant would be ill or die but the caterpillar lives to eat this plant. Something in your belly should be moving, right now. Ever think about what will cause a lily to grow in a desert or valley just to prove the majestic love and power. The caterpillar overeats and attaches itself to the milky leaf (the same plant it eats becomes its life support system) and begins to spin itself into a cocoon and stays until the wings are formed, the legs are dissolved along with most of its body. The plant causes a transformation while enclosed alone in darkness. If interrupted, death would be its end. Though it seems to struggle and needs help, leave it alone. It's being perfected. Today, if you feel you're destined to be a butterfly in your caterpillar state, trust and wait to finish what has begun. It isn't over!!!

DAY 47

To every seed that must bear roots—check the ground in which you're planting your seed. Does the ground have good soil, has it been broken up and will it receive enough sun? Three very important keys to planting your seed are: (1) is this the right season for planting this seed? (2) Do I realize that some seeds take longer to take root and so many seeds you plant this season may cause you to wait another season before they break ground? (3) Name the seed you're planting in the ground, give it time to connect to the ground's surrounding so that it has roots deep enough to be anchored. Part of the cultivation is pulling out weeds, watering, digging around and making adjustments. Then comes the shoot system. It breaks

out of its surrounding and becomes new. No longer just a seed, but now a plant seeking to be more than it started out as and bigger. That seed grows to produce fruit that we are able to be blessed by and live off of. Our seeds need time to become a harvest. Be patient and continue speaking to your seed, it must produce; it has to fulfill its purpose. Love your seed, and say I GOT SEED IN THE GROUND!

DAY 48

Everyone loves to use the words—I love you, but do we know the magnitude of these words, really? How many times have you spoken these words and your heart felt nothing? Has someone told you these words and your heart wanted something it was unable to receive. We're taught that these words have power and can be weapons and tools to almost anything. I remember waiting to hear my dad say those magical words as a young woman, yet they never came. Then seeking out the man that could speak those words made my heart skip a beat and defined my life. Searching for the match of these words can sometimes feel like an endless search. Climbing mountains, swimming oceans, crossing deserts, and flying those friendly skies felt like an endless quest. Then, I understood in order to have love, you must know love and to know it, you must know you. I Love You!

DAY 49

Getting up through the night can prove to be challenging sometimes. We stumble in the dark. Bumping into a wall or door, knocking over this, hitting that toe again and you wonder...I've been walking in this place over and over throughout

the day or in the light with no issues— but in the dark, I become lost in what should be familiar. (Sounds like a parable)?

We are the light of this world. We are not stumbling as those that are in the dark because we are the light. Even when we walk into a new, unfriendly, aggressive, troubled, or evil place, we bring light. We don't have to stumble or be afraid when traveling at night or in darkness because we walk by faith not by sight. Today, we are the walking light in this dark world, let's not stumble or cause others to stumble.

DAY 50

We aren't fighting against human enemies, but against rulers, authorities, forces of cosmic darkness, and spiritual powers of evil in the heavens. Therefore, put on your full armor so that you can stand your ground on the evil day and after you have done everything possible—still stand. Every struggle that we're facing is purposed for us to see life. Our flesh must die and is dying daily—so why do we pamper it. We spend fortunes preserving, beautifying, and satisfying this flesh so much so that we end up losing the purpose of the struggle. Stand through your fight, tears, sickness, and uphill struggles, boundaries and enemies. Our battles are not fleshly but spiritual, so get armored up spiritually to win. Stop wasting time on temporary things and invest in your life spiritually. Stand and win the fight, battle and war that's before you.

DAY 51

From now on, brothers and sisters, if anything is admirable, focus your thoughts on these things: all that is true, all that is just, all that is pure, all that is lovely, and all that is worthy of praise. Live a lifestyle that makes everyone wonder what you are doing that they're not.

Sometimes in your worse places and your most devastated moments you still look like a hero to someone else. So, keep rising to the top, be like the oil that you're made to be; it never loses its power to rise to the top. Some call it the Hustle but you know it to be just a flow. Be great and don't stop.

DAY 52

Our minds will run to and fro with so many thoughts but are they godly ones? Our minds can be dangerous, filled with evil, anger, hatred and ungodly garbage. Someone asked, did I write Nuggets from my heart or copy the words from a book (Lol)? Every nugget I send is original; I don't need anyone to help me express My Heart!

Within each of us are so many great abilities that need to be expressed by song, dance, writings or etc. Our minds are so powerful that it's capable of reaching or falling into many levels. Moments of confusion, challenges, deep hurt, life lessons do combat my thoughts and attempt to cloud my process—yet HOW EXCELLENT..! Clear your mind from the cares, fears and things of the flesh and focus!

DAY 53

Hold your tongue, when you're tempted to say something that you'll later regret. Ever wish you never said that? How you want to take back the pain you sent out? Did you know that hurting people will always hurt others? Sometimes we must be slow to speak yet we must say what we feel, we must defend ourselves, we must put them in their place, we cannot

allow them to feel they won and got the last word. The temptation to speak can cost a price we cannot or desire to pay. Yet the door is always available to get out, be silent, to do well and to choose to spread the good news instead.

Sometimes, our greatest challenge is remaining silent when we have something to say. Our tongue has the power to destroy lives, start a war and build up leaders, while smoothing out contentions. So let us use our tongues to enforce life, touch those in darkness and bringing love to the lonely.

DAY 54

It doesn't matter what someone else says, feels or thinks about you, the question is what you believe about you. Sometimes you may meet those on your journey who feel putting you down makes them superior. Your reality sets the tone for others to accept. If anyone needs to flow in your worth, it is you—others just need to learn the music of your song or reality.

DAY 55

From the beginning of time, we are given choices. A lot of us make choices based on what we are used to and have been accustomed to. In our hearts, we know right from wrong yet why did we still choose that which is wrong before what's right? Today, we must learn that after all that we've done wrong, we're still given us a chance to get it right.

Whatever we've messed up, we can repair; it may time or may just take us making peace with the situation and moving forward.

DAY 56

I listen to the rain this morning; I could only imagine what it would be like if we could receive blessings like this—or do we? Sometimes, we count only the blessings we see, or we feel. What about the ones we don't see? Diseases that could have been terminal; accidents that could have paralyzed; Addictions that could keep our bank accounts cleaned out; contracts on our lives that could have been carried out, our families could have been destroyed in one day; evictions, convictions, home evasion, rape, death, blindness, deaf, mute and the list goes on. Are we grateful? Thankful? Thoughtful? Sorrowful? Giving your best will always assure you will receive the best in return. Let it rain, open the flood gates.

DAY 57

Time is truly on your side. Nothing is hidden forever and anything that we want to know, it will be revealed. The truth is just like oil in water, it always comes to the top. How many nights do we lose crying, worried, stressed and uneasy? It will be revealed; good or bad, it will be revealed. Discernment is a powerful gift. Time is on your side. Remember these words—it will all come out in the wash, everything that done in the dark will come to the light. Whatever you reap, you will sow— a lie will get tired and rest on the truth (that's mine). Your turn, give us a word to confirm it will be revealed.

DAY 58

Too deep with truth! The world is setting up its kingdom here on earth, as it is written. Our world will destroy itself;

time is winding up, pay attention. Too many things are being excused that should be corrected and dealt with.

Our enemies are rallying up all their forces while we're talking loud and not interceding. As our enemies are making their stand, we are cowardly nodding in agreement because we would rather be popular than right. Open your eyes and mouth; stand up for truth; no matter who it offends. When we know who we are; the head not the tail (we lead, not follow). We understand that leaders are few, followers are many. Our Kingdom will come…the world is not our Kingdom, don't be deceived. Wake-up and stand up for what is right and stop cosigning on the lies. This is not an easy pill to swallow but truth comes that way sometimes.

DAY 59

Have you met anyone always talking about their dreams, want and wish, but NEVER expressing how hard they're willing to work for it? Sometimes I am approached by strangers asking for money for food, gas, or whatever, you too; I imagine. My response is—are you willing to work for it? Money didn't come to me freely. Why am I expected to give it away so freely? Before you grunt—yes there are times I will freely give, if I am moved. Are you really helping or hindering? Teach a man to fish…you know the phrase. We must work our faith, we must be willing to sometimes get dirty, talked about and possibly ostracized but still pushing to reach our goals. Write it down, put together the plan then work it, so how bad do you want it?

DAY 60

Repeated phrases may be redundant to some but needed by others. I'm one that hates to repeat myself yet find myself doing it more times than I wish to. I know it is important at times to repeat something for clarity and to remind ourselves of the task at hand. Whether on a job, with a person, in a lifestyle, a habit, place, organization or etc., sometimes repetition is necessary. If I'm unable to praise, talk about, live and portray what's within me, around me or what's runs through me, IT IS NOT WORTH LOSING YOURSELF OVER. (Repeat)

Our spirit is trying to show and tell us something, if we choose to grab hold of the knowledge in us. Choose wisely who you'll serve, connect to and allow in your atmosphere. The only reason we're entering darkness is to bring it to the light. We should not be stumbling out there when our light is bright. Awesome to repeat, are we listening?

DAY 61

Time! Sometimes it's wasted, not valued or given as planned. If we could do anything different, most would change our wasted time. When you go for any business transactions, they need it written. You must sign your check, fill out an application, apply for a loan, car, house, employment and etc. Writing allows us to see our goal. Before you can hit a target, you must first see it. Once you can see it, then you can move towards it. Every day, we should be moving towards our goal. Without a vision (goal) the people (us) perish. Once you write your goals, then you must work, yes; work to achieve them with no peanut gallery interruptions. ANYONE, ANYTHING, OR ANYWHERE THAT TAKES US FROM WHAT IS WRITTEN (PLAN) IS NOT THE DIRECTION WE NEED

TO TAKE. Our vision is clear when our goals are written and directed. What time is it in your life?

DAY 62

You can't rest until you have landed. Many times, we can have plenty of great ideas and things going on in our lives but how many unfinished projects do we have now? We start on songs, books, missions, savings, relationships and the lists continue and pause to work on something else. Our ancestors say, "We got too many irons in the fire", choose one and complete it.

I can start to clean up my living room and take something into the kitchen; then I'm working in the kitchen; what happened to the work I began in the living room? Of course, I plan on getting back to the first project but right now I'm detained by another one. Can anyone else identified? Land!

DAY 63

People can tell you anything about themselves, but associates tell it better. He or she may come off one way—take another glimpse, look or observe the associates they keep, they can't be played off. You know. Birds of a feather flock together. You're identified by the company you keep. It's real. They may seem sweet, religious, loving, and good; however, check out the company they choose to keep. Let's make it more personal than that, check out your birds that you choose to flock with. Yep—we've might have more zeros than heroes. Hmm. If you chose more wishers than believers; more talkers than doers; more losers than winners; more complainers than conquerors, and more "ain'ts than saints"— the problem is not

them—it's you. It's hard to make a long prosperous journey with dead weight.

DAY 64

Imagine within each of us is so many possibilities that we've not tapped into. Whether we're 5 or 105, it's never too late or early. Within us is the ability to do something that everyone wished they had done or thought of. Our challenge is that many of us fear the next move, have no confidence in self, believe it's either too early or too late and many just abort the assignment. Yes, we've all been given an assignment to bring into this world. Some have been given several. Many times, we sit on our assignments, meddling in someone else's. Other times, we procrastinate until when we decide to move—the space is taken. There are those who always need someone else to push, pay, believe or do it for them. Take your assignment and run. It is delivered. Pregnancy is a clear understanding that life is within you waiting and desiring to come forth. Aborting the assignment or pregnancy is a great loss that can't be duplicated. Miscarrying is an indication something is wrong and cannot go any further. Pregnancy is the beginning of a delivery. Can you follow through on the possibilities within YOU? Peep into your sonogram (future) and know life awaits you. Can you guess what it is?

DAY 65

Have you ever wondered what happened to the dreamers that slept and the visionaries that succeeded? You can have sleepless nights or wishing and dreaming but unable to reach life's journey. —Or you can set up a plan with the Master plan

and walk into your life's destiny. Most of the time, the answer is with the connection. Who are you connected with? Ever meet the famous, "I'm going to people?" Always going but never gone. Procrastinators are seemingly always in quicksand. They make moves, but sink. Check out their connection, those who they choose to surround themselves in the company of.

On the other hand—the visionaries (my eagles) they get something in sight and traveling alone is almost the only way they fly. The word never is not in their vocabulary. The visionary carefully makes allowance for the vision to come to pass. There may be delays, battles and presses, but giving up or in isn't the answer. When they do find another eagle that will assist in the vision, it's unstoppable force and true victory. Don't give time to a dream killer that'll keep you away from the plan. Lighten up your load and train with other visionaries that can see pass yesterday, will be in the work of today as you reap the wealth of tomorrow. Ever see an eagle fly low to feed a chicken? So why do we stop to entertain those that are positioned only to slow us up instead of assisting our soar—Million-dollar mind with pennies in the bank. Have you seen one or are you one?

DAY 66

Today we recognize that our days are filled with so many decisions, choices, attacks, evil, excitement, hurt, teachers, experiences, regrets, praise, accomplishments and the list go on. We become busy, drained, restless, amused, stressed, lost and etc until finding a place of rest, devotion; gratification and love for just you become ridiculously low. We're caught up with the news, our children, semi friends, social media, personal

issues and we really don't use the true time that we deserve. Thinking about the times, we could've or should've lost our life, been in the psych ward or serving life in prison but our ground changed. I am learning to value time more each day and not to be consumed by others ignorance or judgments of what is going on in my life.

DAY 67

Faith says, "I am never alone, and I'm not discouraged by what it looks like". I shall fulfill every word that has been spoken over my life. So, declare to every storm that may be raging in or around you right now—I'm not alone. Every blow that has hit you has identified your power to stand, overcome, endure, suffer and WIN.

I don't how your Faith has been tested but we must know that we'll find out just how deep our faith is when it's being challenged. Can we believe when everything we see is a lost, confusing and a failure? Remember, as long as we got Faith, we're never alone. That door, storm, situation, breakup and disaster isn't the end, it's what needed to bring us before Faith. Stand on your Faith and don't bulge!

DAY 68

Can we leap first? Are we able to begin packing before we know where we are going? Can we walk away from a job start our own business? Most of us of capable of talking about our plans but few have mastered the skills to carry them out. Leaping and believing your wings will come in the faith attempt. How awesome is that? Taking the leap of Faith! Whatever we're believing for; car, home, job, business, ministry,

family, debt, sickness, troubles—Leap into, onto, through, to and from it. Nothing is stopping you but you.

DAY 69

Pressure, pressing, suppress, oppress and depression. Leon Baily has quoted the saying, "Too much pressure burst pipes."

There are so many pressures we're challenged with and by each day. Our children, relationships, health, finances, mental state, spiritual life and influences all connect to some form of pressure. Pressure must be relieved, how? Through our Faith and trusting that everything has its timing we can be brought to breakthroughs instead of breakdowns. When we get to it, we must choose to go through it. Break chains, curses and work it out, release the pressure. Let's not work so hard to get out of the pressures that suffocate us, just let go and receive our breakthrough.

DAY 70

Let's study to be quiet and to do your own business. Study to be quiet! Why? How many times have you wished you didn't say what you said? The poison that can flow from our minds onto our tongues cannot be erased—so study to be quiet, listen more, talk less—shh -listen to our inner voice more and then wait to tell it. Words do and can hurt us—even more than sticks and stones.

Most of us feel, if we can't tell it then it wouldn't be told correctly, or we can't allow someone to get by with talking to or about us like they do. But we feel we must defend ourselves and speak; only to find out later that our words caused more

damage than rectifying. Silence can be golden.

DAY 71

The impossible can be possible, if you press and believe. There may be a slim chance you'll get the loan, make it through school, recover from an illness, see them again, win in court, give birth, find a real woman/man, win the award, publish a best seller, meet destiny on the first try, own a fortune 500 company, see your name in lights in Hollywood and etc. It's slim—but possible. When they say it's slim or no chance; choose the slim. It seemed slim, but as the story goes Moses, David, the Three Hebrew boys, Sarah and Ruth had slim chances that became big opportunities to show out. There are no odds against us when we will strive to do the impossible.

DAY 72

Are you limitless or limited? Imagine all your life doing the same thing yet inside knowing you were created to do more. Not settling for the things that are in your reach but exploring those things that haven't been discovered yet. Going to work each day and dreaming of something better. It's in us to achieve greater works, promise with greater power.

Our lives should reflect Our God or Higher Power; more than anything else. Can someone see you beholding the glory and taking an ordinary situation and making an awesome outcome? Become limitless, full of possibilities and visions. When someone says that you can't do it, be it, see it, or excel in it, remember there's a bigger Power than you who has NO LIMITS! You can do it, pursue it, challenge it, overtake it and master it because it's your impossible. Live in the IMPOS-

SIBLE, speak to the INVISIBLE, take hold of the INTANGIBLE and believe the INCREDIBLE. We're only one page, step, move, letter, answer, day, delay, person, invention, miracle, door, home, paycheck and love from our destiny.

DAY 73

Why we are on a bar stool when the reclining chair is much more comfortable? They say if we knew better, we would do better, would we? Is there a price for ignorance? Of course, how many times have we said, If I knew or I wish I knew that? Why? Because the price we pay for not knowing before we signed the papers, before we chose to commit, before we did, said, went etc. Then ask yourself –were you fully ignorant or just resistant in learning or knowing? How many times did someone try to tell you something, guide you somewhere, introduce you to someone and we refused? Sometimes you can refuse to know because blindness works better for you. As we mature and become wiser; we see the ditch and avoid it. We carefully exhibit a sign for others. They see the sign, examine the ditch and brace for the jump, figure that one. Don't believe everyone is ready to know, because you're not sure that you do. But when you know that you know that you know, seek greater wisdom on how to teach others.

DAY 74

We question many things in our lives. Including why did this happen to me? What did I do to deserve this? What's wrong with me? Why am I here? Where am, I supposed to be? Who can I trust or go to? What do I suppose to do or where do I go? Some questions are not answered. Some are

answers we do not want, and some leave us still in tears. We must truly trust our purpose even when we don't see it. We must rely on it when we don't see it, when we can't feel it, follow it when we don't' know what it is. Through pain, discomfort, let downs, separation, loss and despair, we're still winners and know that it's ALL working for our good. There's no oops in the plan nor exempt from the world's lows but they cannot touch our mountain highs. It isn't over until it's over. We've got protectors all around us working, shielding, interceding, holding, loving, and moving.

DAY 75

One of the greatest changes we must make is our communication line. The reason, purpose, power, and quality of our spiritual communication are so important. Prayer (divine communication) is our weapon in battle, our intimate time with our inner spirit, our strength, our peace, our ability to touch heaven, friends, family, strangers, and things.

It is a greater source of healing, forgiving, believing, and even forgetting. We pray in tears, laughter, songs, groaning and in silence. Prayer doesn't see prejudice, status, origin, boundaries, and impossibilities—it sees Faith. Many say all I can do is pray about it. What they really should say is—I'll pray because that's the key, the answer and the connection. Whenever prayer touches our universe, something must change, got to change, and has changed. So, change your prayer life and your life will change.

DAY 76

When our very foundation is shaken, it may seem as though there is no hope and all is lost, we feel like we've been snagged by our worse fears, overwhelmed with bills, stressed by life's woes, challenged by doctor's reports, setup to fail and struggling with the relationship at hand. What is the correct decision, right move and direct approach? Look up! Look up and know that our life is totally awesome—is not insecure, shaken, restless, fearful, disabled, discombobulated, poor, miserable or anything less than great. Look up! We must be ready to fight our battles, mend our hearts, speak into our future, direct our paths, fill our cups, restore our peace, love, joy and grace, encourage us, guide our feet, decrease our worries and shake our foundation!! When the foundation is shaken, there must be a move that releases every grip that attempted to delay, discourage, confuse, manipulate, destroy and steal the plans for our lives. We don't need to react to the enemy; we must rely on, rest in and release the power over every situation. When our foundation is shaken, let's study to show ourselves approved so we can maintain an A. We must work on being the greatest we can be when failure is not an option.

DAY 77

If we can be faithful over the little, we will be ready to be the ruler over much. Don't complain about what you don't have, be grateful for what you do have. There are people out there who are worse off than us and wish they could have what we got. Take care of the little things so that we can be blessed with even greater things.

Many times, we're so busy trying to get something that we're not appreciating what we already have. Wash that old

car, keep it clean, maintain your home with its imperfections and one day you'll see doors open for more. There's has to be a place of contentment and satisfaction so we can enjoy our lives to its fullest. Be a great and faithful steward and there's no limit to what we can possess, once we've proven to be worthy.

DAY 78

I'm not exempted! Sometimes when bad things happen in our lives, we feel we've been picked on, yet it is life making its rounds. When bad things happen, when sickness comes, family issues, lied on and talked about. We will be hated, misunderstood, fail, have addictions, mental battles, financial woes, repossessions, foreclosures, death, be broken hearted, unforgiven, abused, demoted and so forth. Why do we feel we should be exempt? Reading about the story of Joseph this morning—sometimes you're chosen to be the one to go through hell. What was the charge? He was born by a mother that his father loved so much he made him a colorful coat that signified everywhere he went that he was special, or I want to use the word favored. Felt that? Yes, your attacks are to prove how special you are. It shows that you have the favor over your life. Hospital couldn't hold us, doctors couldn't sentence us, judges couldn't convict us, lies couldn't stop us and weapons can't kill us. Not exempted—just favored. Say so!

DAY 79

Arising early this morning upon meditating on this thought we are flesh, living as a spiritual being (god-like) and wonder why our biggest battle is with ourselves. Do you remember that it was in heaven, that the first war of good and

evil, who really won? Evil was able to turn 1/3 of the good angels to bad or evil, in what period of time? Let's take a look of evil; it comes looking right for the wrong reasons. The test of the tree in the garden is another prime example of having evil is always present, available and eager to please. Fall back?

If we're obedient, many of us could avoid some battles, mishaps and broken hearts but we normally enjoy just doing things our way and then deal with the consequences. Sometimes, the war breaks out in our homes, workplace, and relationships and yes even in our churches but know that our spirit knows how to win. Anything or anyone that you lose in our transformation must be declared the sacrifice for the maintenance of our spiritual cleaning. Inside each of us; there is still a war of good and evil, who is winning?

DAY 80

Balance is something that we should seek at all times. Most of us can tell when our balance is off; physically, spiritually, emotionally, mentally, socially or financially.

When our internal indicators begin to show or tell us that we're imbalanced; we need to take inventory. Anyone or anything that we bring into our lives should help in our balance not against it. If, we're off balance becuz of something or someone; adjust accordingly.

Have you ever had a wonderful day and it took one call, text, visit or interruption to throw us off the grid? It's becuz they've tipped the scale; this tip could be critical or fatal, so let's work on being aligned.

Meditation, yoga, walking, eating healthier and having a peaceful environment with peaceful people is essential.

DAY 81

Lessons are given to us free-what are we learning from them? We are given cheat sheets, but we choose not to use them. Our cheat sheets are all the information we have around us to assist us in living and doing better. Whenever we are approached with a lesson, we can either get more information or bypass it and learn our own lesson. Some lessons are expensive, so are heartbreaking, some are destructive, some leave ugly scars, lifetime issues, major inabilities to trust, blindness, deaf and continuous circles of same old same ole. When do we tire of seeing the same things, people, and circumstances at different times, faces and covers but the same results? Insanity! Same game, different players, same places, different addresses, same words, different voices.

It's time to begin a new journey that bypasses the lies, confusion, setups, ignorance and paths of destruction. Giants will keep coming, your enemies are sent to be your foot stool—not your yoke. Break the curse on people from your life while your door is open, and you possess the keys. Everyone is a blessing in our lives—we just need to know how.

DAY 82

Let's have peace when storms are raging and allow us to remember we are here to protect, provide, decide, guide, interrupt, empower, educate, build, break, use, heal, deliver, sacrifice, lift, love, deny, touch and the list is endless. There's always something we must combat in order to keep our peace. Peace is a valuable fruit to possess and if you don't believe its essential; lose it and find out how life changes.

We can have all the money needed but without peace, the money can't keep us happy or satisfied. I've lived in the most

desirable homes, possess the best of materialistic things but without peace; I couldn't enjoy them. I walked away from lifestyles that most dream of because there was no peace in it. Never lose your peace for anything or anyone because it'll be the very jewel needed in any situation. Seek peace and guard it with your full being.

DAY 83

Some things we have no control over for a reason. It seems life has a wonderful sense of humor when we're allowed to be neighbors with a testimony. Let's clarify testimony, it's not telling how our enemy has won but it is a test you've overcame. Our neighbor can be states away but can still be the test we need to make us better, brighter, and closer to our purpose.

Have you ever felt like you can't take anymore, and you want to lay everything down and take matters into your own hands and yet somehow bound by tears, frustrations, sometimes even humiliation; you stand tall.

We will find that neighbor was planted in our lives for purpose; not to destroy us, as they'd hoped—but to teach us. Be grateful for every neighbor, far and near, good and bad, loving and hateful, fruit and nuts—it's all working for our good. Love every root of hell in them is our power.

DAY 84

When you desire to reach higher platforms, expect the lower levels of the enemy to attack. There is always some enemy watching and waiting for the opportunity to take us down. We must know they are mostly inside not outside of our circle. It's hard to find out your weakness unless you allow someone

to get close enough to see it. Go higher, reach out of the limits of this world and soar the atmosphere.

Most of our enemies have no desire to fly; it's too demanding and uses up too much energy. Their efforts are to discourage us from moving forward, becoming stagnant and depressed so will give up. Remain focused. Your enemies can't hold, touch, or curse you, unless you stop moving and believing. Stand on the Greater and go higher.

DAY 85

If things don't seem to be working out as we desire or planned; it's okay to try another approach or change things. Sometimes it only takes us to change; become divergent. We can't control how someone treats us, yet we do control how we treat them. Have we ever thought about the best way to help someone could be to just walk away, close the door, or say nothing? Sacrifice is to give up something you want to keep. Think about it, if it didn't hurt letting it go, it wasn't a sacrifice, and the battle remains. Know that we are created to be unique and many times that is not accepted, it's okay.

Love who, what, where and how we've been made to be. It may make others uncomfortable, competitive, jealous or place you alone, yet our change has come; the world is our stepping stone. I'll be divergent, how about you? Having power to do it all will always be a threat to many, a puzzle to others and a blessing to the rest. Divergent!

DAY 86

Never allow anyone to stunt your growth, you are bigger than that. Anyone who desires to remind you of your

past shortcomings, failures, sins, hurts, faults or mistakes –is choosing to live in their past—not yours. You have overcome those things through grace, mercy and forgiveness. Those who are trying to watch your past may find that difficult. Watching your smoke is easier because there is a fire in your future. Trust that! Your future is so much brighter than the past. Introductions may not be necessary; growth speaks for itself and it's looking awesome on you. The enemy seeks to accuse and destroy you because of your past. Our promises are the plans of a prosperous future. Live in the future. It's far brighter.

DAY 87

Sometimes, we find ourselves complaining over and over about the very thing we alone can change. Whatever we are looking at in our mirrors is our true reflection. If what we see about ourselves isn't pleasing, guess who has the power to change it? Us. If we are not happy with our lives, relationships, bodies, attitudes, choices, jobs, finances, environment, spiritual reflection etc., let's do something that brings better results. Stop complaining about the problem and let's begin to be the solution. Complaining doesn't get us closer but many times further away. No one enjoys a complainer, and your company will be fewer because it's not enriching or encouraging for anyone to listen. To want better, you must first believe you are well able to possess greater.

DAY 88

If you are lonely, where are you? You're possibly at the top. You can always find a crowd at the bottom. They're the

complainers, drama filled, liars, deceivers, back biters, haters, miserable, unfulfilled, troublemakers, envious, regular etc. Instead of climbing out of the pack that refuses to work on #1; themselves, they'll sit and stir up trouble in every listening ear. If every time you turn, someone is spewing your name out of their mouth, rejoice. If people find contempt in just having to be in your presence, make it a lasting impression. If you got them rolling their eyes, fuming at the mouth and near to an anxiety attack; praise God that you've been chosen to drench in this power.

It may get lonely, but the air is sweeter, the view is spectacular and the benefits are out of this world. You choose to climb, when others sat. You chose to work on your own self and not live on or off others. You found what a true asset was and became one. You used the bridges instead of mumbling about the steps. Don't look down or you could possibly fall back into what you fought so hard to get out of. Be careful how you extend your hand—you may be trying to pull up someone whose purpose is to bring you back down.

DAY 89

There are many losses to the procrastinator. How many times have we lost opportunities, careers, friends, potential mates, assets, answers etc. just because we thought we could handle it later? Our later becomes Never. I'll call them tomorrow and they left today. I'll take care of it later and it is lost now. I'll explain why I did that later, but the friendship ended because of the lack of communication. The need to apologize later should've been done earlier. He or she is in town and wants to get up with you—yet you're too busy doing nothing that you missed an opportunity of a lifetime.

How many blessings were in our now that we felt could or would wait for us? Love, embrace, apologize, be honest, be open, remain friendly, alert, prayerful, forgiving, drop habits that are harmful, people that cause drama, problems that bring stress and anxiety, close doors to pain, hurts, hate and lies; and do it all NOW. Don't be a procrastinator!

DAY 90

Where does or did the time go? Time waits for no one and once it is gone, it's not returning. How much time in our day was just wasted? I can play a game for hours, when there is so many things needing my attention—how about you? Have you ever caught yourself in the middle of a sentence and realized you've said it time and time again? I'm tired of you treating me this way. If you do that again, I'm going to …? I can't take this anymore? I'm just going to quit? I am not doing that no more. That's my last time. I'm going to leave—alone. I'll read today. I'll do it tomorrow. I'm done. And the list goes on and so does time.

We can't stop time, but we can stop ignoring it purpose. Use it wisely. Rise early and seek guidance so your day isn't wasted. Rise. Shine. Give time the respect needed, and it'll reward you throughout the day!

DAY 91

The moment we set our foot out of our homes, what is the goal? Do we walk out with the mindset— "I'm going out to proclaim and declare my purpose" or do we go out with the mindset, "I do not have the patience for people today." Have you ever looked at the trees, seas, and animals, any creation

and told it that it is good? Seems a little crazy; right? No, because everything has a voice; whether we can understand it or not.

When we woke up this morning, were we ready to be the best that we can be regardless of any obstacles, situations or ailments? There's always an opportunity to do so. How many people can we reach out to today to lend a helping hand to? How much time are we willing to invest in others to succeed? Who do we truly work for? Are our plans for today based on truth and setting great goals?

DAY 92

Most of us are guilty of this very distracting and addictive problem. There are days that I purposefully leave my cell phone at home as I pull out of my driveway. Why? Because I don't want anything I couldn't live without in this world that will keep me from entering the new world. Cell phones aren't bad. What we do with them, can be. How many break ups, arguments, fights, killings, gossiping, setups, recordings, pictures etc. has been behind the use of the cell phone. Ever wonder why it's now free so that every adult can have one, really? And we can't wait for our children to be able to hold one and make sure they get one by kindergarten, for what purpose?

Our children are just as distracted as us and we've got no idea who we've connected them to, or what we have connected them to. School teachers can't teach because they are checking their cells too. Observe, then ask ourselves, if the cell is replacing our ability to communicate? They say it takes 21 days to start a habit—can we take a day to break this one?

DAY 93

When we learn to forgive, it'll enlarge our view while remaining focused on the target. When you are a lion; a conqueror (King or Queen)—how do you find time to focus on those who can't stop your flow? It's like an 18-wheeler facing a Volkswagen—no fear. It is like a whale against a goldfish—no fear. What about a tornado heading towards a hummingbird—no fear.

Whatever been sent to destroy us needs to know we don't fear it, we believe in our Protector, Strong Tower and Deliverer. We've been given several death threats, medical diagnoses, evictions, breakup and emotional setbacks but NO Fear! Our enemies are against us—no fear. Our past attacking our future (Jeremiah 29:11). No fear!!! No Weapon form against us shall prosper…No Fear.

DAY 94

What we do should be our passion. Many of us are doing what we don't love. Why? We do it for the sake of convenience, money, circumstances, inheritance, unskilled etc. This has us out of alignment with our purpose, passion and plan. Time and focus can place us back in position with what we enjoy doing. Let's find ourselves loving what we do because what we do, we love.

Let's find our passion and go after it without hesitation or regret. Within in our passion is our purpose to fulfill great Leaders who lead by example make better teacher.

DAY 95

Simply put, obedience can bring us blessings. From the very beginning of our lives, we are taught to be obedient. We can have whatever we desire if we're obedient and /or follow instructions. Sometimes just following instructions is the very thing that can get us into great doors, wellness and life changing experiences.

I know we can look back at the moments in our lives in which we weren't obedient and it cost us a price that we weren't happy to pay. Our parents or love ones try to tell us things so we could avoid the heartaches, pains, disappointments and hard knocks we chose to encounter. Can we imagine how many roads, opportunities and situations we could have avoided if we had listened to wise instructions and were obedient? Today, let's be more in tune with our spiritual life that we can hear when to, how to, who to and where to? Obedience is better than sacrifice!

DAY 96

Have you ever met someone was completely dishonest, unfair, irresponsible, immature and lost yet got others backing them up? It's like watching someone stand outside in a thunderstorm under a tree cursing out the Higher Powers and beside them is that person screaming, "Say it again." It like someone recording another person committing a horrendous act, who's worse—the one committing it or the one who takes joy in filming it?

Don't admire a fool or you will be foolish. If you see a fool digging a grave for them— don't grab a shovel and dig yours too. We've been given great nuggets in our lives to cause us to be overcome, achieve, resist and be powerful; let's use them.

DAY 97

Ever wonder how you got that stain on your clothes? What did you rub up against? Who touched you with unclean hands and will it come out? Everyday we're surrounded by things, people and places that will or can get us dirty. Our minds battle unclean thoughts, our words speaking untruths and our hearts denying perfect love. So, today let's create (make, design) in me a clean (clear from dirt, spotless), heart (that knows agape love, doesn't alter from purity). Then change my twisted, confused, depressed, limited and closed mind so my spirit can be and remain new and righteous. When we are off course, let's be guided because we need to restored, revived, revealed, and repelled.

We are leaning towards the correct instructions so that we may obey. Oh, whatever, wherever, or whoever has or will cause us to be unclean—wash us so we can be more pure.

DAY 98

Putting our requests and desires into the atmosphere has the greatest power at anytime, anyplace, any way and for/to anyone. Have you ever claimed something through Faith and later begin to doubt the very thing you were professing? Either we're going to stand on it or complain about it? Faith puts strength in our weaknesses, love against the haters, joy when sorrow is knocking, miracles out of messes, sight to the blind, wealth coming out of poverty and leaders that stop following.

Remember when we make stands, it means we will be faced with resistance but we must remain vigilant, strong and powerful. Sometimes our vision is blurred by so many false plays, players and lies but maintain the stance anyway.

DAY 99

Examine your power by the battles you've entered into and stood against the forces that be. What is the purpose in having power if we're not using it or being tested on it? How many times have we thought that we couldn't handle this or that until we're facing it? Then we find out that though we wish we didn't have to encounter the ordeal, we did find that our inner power is always ready.

Within us a greater power that when we can no longer do it, hold or believe; it illuminates. We are so Solar, able to absorb the power and light up, charge, bring a great force whenever it's needed. Most can't understand it or know how to use it but when we seek it, we'll find it; alive and ready! So seek it and you'll know the truth of power.

DAY 100

The person that's making trails can go much further on their feet than on their butt. We can sit and watch the world go around or stand and create footprints for others to follow. We must get up and begin moving so others may know how to follow. We may not be the one to complete the vision but the trail can easily be picked up. Gliding across the country from a sitting position can be quite painful—slow and with many blisters.

Rise up and put to work the plan that will cause us to go on journeys to fulfill our destiny and build landmarks for others to follow. Mind your footprints, someone will follow.

DAY 101

When we say we're children of A Higher Power (God), some reflections must be evident. One is the ability to hold it together when situations look dim. How? Put some light on it; your light is the only way of bringing things out and revealing anything hidden.

If you're still not convinced—look around and you can find someone who can say, "I know there's a Power bigger in me." Our enemy will always present a lie, fear and a wide street of let's do our own thing; to keep us in darkness. Remember, there are no new tricks just new participants. Don't panic, we're covered, trust your guide, we'll shine through our situation. We've been made bigger than any problem, question, circumstance, bill, Doctor's report, loss or anything for that matter.

DAY 102

And at Midnight ...I am awakened with this powerful and Never to be forgotten word. We're included in the whole wide world (our www) which includes the good, bad, and ugly.

We desire to love the www and want the www to love us back, but realistically we see our world has been engulfed with much hate and war. There are times we struggle to love our family, spiritual sisters and brothers, our fellow races, enemies, exes, abusers, accusers, oppressors, government officials, co-workers etc.

It's a wake-up call. You may not need it because your love is perfect but I am embracing this with a new mind, clean heart and bucket of tears. We've got to truly get it together or not.

DAY 103

The worse thing that has happened to us didn't destroy us. So, keep going, tear down all barriers, destroy all doubt, kill all dream killers and eliminate all fear because our life, peace, joy and hope is in A Higher Power. Keep moving forward; disappointed—move, hurt—move, struggling—move, lonely—move, whatever, whoever, wherever—keep moving. It's hard to hit a moving target, don't be a sitting duck but remain soaring eagle. No worries, all gain; it's all good.

DAY 104

Can you imagine being handed an assignment that immediately makes you feel doomed? Being born with Destiny's purpose means that you have and assignment that may not be comfortable, reasonable, recognizable or durable yet it's the assignment we must complete. How many successors were born in poverty, abandoned, rejected and totally loss? Yet their destiny didn't line up with their struggles but faith out grew it all.

We're assigned, people, places and things that we may not enjoy, could cause pain and suffering is a key component. Many times it's in the suffering that we find our way, get our release and leave grave sites of our old selves. Ever notice how ugly a duckling is before it becomes a swan? Be faithful over the little and watch greater be performed.

DAY 105

Somehow our character is always being checked and observed, so let's make sure we're operating in our Integrity. One of our greatest values is our character. Many can perform but true character cannot be put on stage or swim in a glass bowl without causing value and worth.

Who we are is measured within by the scales of life not by what we attempt to convince others of about us. How many can say that you know someone who is on their Sunday's best yet struggle Monday-Saturday? Be of great character and Integrity wherever, whenever and whoever. Our character can take and get us into many places that we couldn't be in without it.

So let's build up our character and a have a positive outlook and awesome impression on a somewhat dark world.

DAY 106

In life, we're given so many choices; what we decide to do with them is another story. We can choose to follow the rules or not; in knowing there's consequences when we're not in unison with what's right. We can reap the benefits of being obedient or the hardships of walking contrary to this.

We make choices that can build or destroy us, bring or send, have love or hate; so be mindful of each one you make.

DAY 107

How many times have somebody told you the answer to the madness they're about to walk into, trying to scramble out of or prayed they'll live through it? Yet, even with fair warn-

ing, we still walk directly in the line of fire. Wisdom many times comes with a price that has to be paid for, needs to be educated about, we must travel roads to get to or lose everything because of it.

Don't we wish we had listened? Instead, we believed we had a monopoly to the game—only to find we're a part of the game plan. If there's a way to get knowledge that will only cost us an attentive ear—listen. Wisdom isn't cheap, so let's absorb its worth through others wisdom instead of doing another foolish move.

DAY 108

Gratitude allows us to be content with what we don't have. Otherwise, we will be struggle and stressing about the cares of this world. Ever try to satisfy someone who can't be satisfied? It's like trying to fill a pot with no bottom; a description of hell for most people (bottomless pit).

Let's try to become full and satisfied so there is so much more room ahead. We'll never reach the higher level if we are not wise with the ones we have now.

DAY 109

Ever felt like you were winning… life was going well and then suddenly it felt like a monkey jumped on your back? It seems that nothing is going right and you're on the losing end. As in the movie The Color Purple—maybe God is trying to tell you something. You're searching for peace, a breakthrough, a helping hand, a change; maybe you have an Achan in your life, home or business.

Achan was an Israelite (a chosen people) but he was dis-

obedient to the instructions that he was given. Disobedience can and most of the times cause us a dilemma, somewhere down the road. If things are looking bitter instead of better; let's check our camp. Sometimes you got to be ready to lose a friend, partner, or relationship to be blessed away from the curse. Ever notice that your connection may need to be disconnected? Don't be afraid to let the Achan go or prepare to lose everything: battles, promises, prosperity, family or whatever could be the next step. Some people start off good and turn bad, some played good but were always bad. Some just want your good or goods. If things are going wrong, do an Achan check. They call that place Anchor Valley, not a coincidence: anchors hold you back and down.

We are destined for the Greater things. Sometimes we are the weight and other times we are carrying dead weight. Release the anchor.

DAY 110

When the worse most hurtful or unexpected blow makes, your heart hurt, mind spin and body buckle; remember it's not what you are served, it's what you do with it. I feel the sourer the lemons, the sweeter the lemonade. Don't allow the lemons to define your next move, stage, relationship or destiny. Just make sure you bring the sugar, your love, your strength and your Faith. Our Faith has as much power as what we give it. We've been equipped with everything we'll need to make every lemon produce the sweetest lemonade.

The challenge is to make our best and sweetest lemonade whenever we're given the sourest lemons.

DAY 111

Have we ever gone looking for an answer that has already been provided to us inside our heart? Yet, we question our heart, spirit and insight from either the lessons we've encountered or those around us that have discouraged us. Most of our answers are already instilled within us, if we take the time to seek it. Why does it sometime become almost the last place we look instead of the first?

Trust the guide that has been place in us and carefully designed to lead us, assist us in our purpose.

DAY 112

"If you don't like what you're reaping, you had better change what you have been sowing."

J. Rohn

Just remember—whatever the battle— you're on the winning team. Don't look at your hands; trust the team that we're connected to. Whatever seems to be crushing, worrying, attacking, tormenting, discouraging, hating or angering you, remember we're on the winning team.

You can't lose unless you give up, give in or fail to believe. We are much stronger than we know, wiser than we believe and got more love and patience than we thought possible.

We're reaping and sowing all the time, look at our fields, check the harvest and know our hands were included; good, bad or indifferent. Remember we're an army of blazing fire, loving arms and wise Elders; there's no worries needed, we got this.

DAY 113

Integrity will simply reveal our character. Our lifestyle can show the image of who we are, at whatever stage we're in; especially when it's adorned with Integrity. Integrity isn't who we portray ourselves to be when others are watching, but when you are alone. I'm a firm believer that we can mask for a while but who we are in public is many times a reflection of who we want to be looked upon by others but isn't necessarily the truth. Our integrity is on display 24/7/365 in our home, workplace, social networks, society, dates etc. If our integrity is being questioned, we may want to examine ourselves closer. We spend too much time examining others that we miss our own flaws. Let's polish up our integrity and leave no questions asked on how we choose to walk in our integrity; regardless. Is our integrity trustworthy?

DAY 114

We might be spending too time complaining, being angry or holding someone hostage with unforgiveness. If we're doing right, it'll turn out right as well as if we are doing wrong, expect wrong to follow. The law of the universe; whether it's in secret or open the assurance of reaping is guaranteed. Do what you know to be good in our sowing and you'll love the result of the reaping. Think about it, as much as it pains us to confess truth, look at the life we've lived and then inhale the harvest.

As much as we don't want to admit it, we've fallen short by doing some wrong things such as; victimizing others, taking advantages of others and praying that our seeds would die before it gets root. Let's learn to plant good seeds today and accept the reaping of tomorrow. Seed, Time & Harvest:

DAY 115

Many times, we don't have a say in what life throws at us, but we can have a say in what we do with what is thrown. Sounds funny? But think about it. Whatever we welcome, introduce and make comfortable in our life, doesn't seem to bother us until it becomes a problem.

Ever look at someone and ask; how come they can't see a person for what they are doing and who they are? It's hard to smell bad odor when we're tangled in it. Most people are robbed by someone they know and given access to their lives. In order to be betrayed by someone, they must first have to snuggle close at some point. Stay mindful and focused.

DAY 116

We have no control over what is handed to us but we can control what we do with it. When we set our mind, heart, life, soul and vision for greatness, it's not coming without a price. Are we willing to pay that price? If we desire a new car, to further our education, a five-star vacation or great relationship, think about the price, sacrifices, work and many obstacles before us.

Within a year, there will be storms, battles, disappointments, sickness, pain, triumphs, wealth and delays in our lives. Adjust, revise, rethink and press forward because destiny waits. If it's going to be big, then so must be the ship we sail—so expect the winds to change but remaining on course is the reward.

DAY 117

The very thing that keeps us in trouble many times is freedom. Freedom to say, feel, act and think as we want. With this Freedom: Freewill demands responsibility and accountability from us. We can do anything we want in most instances, we can, but do we? We have the power to win battles that are impossible, to live in a place that you couldn't afford but what do we do?

We can do so much when we're connected to A Higher Power that stretches us to activate what's invested in us. We can choose the negative things of this world that can keep us in a vicious cycle of frustration or seek to move it, change it, stop it and rearrange it. We are supplied with that power.

If we want to quit a bad habit, give up some negative ways, be healed from past relationships, sicknesses, mental or emotional illnesses, walk out of poverty into prosperity; we can.

DAY 118

We're constantly battling with our weight, what to do or don't, what to eat or not, who's the best for us, etc. Our bodies come in many forms and yet we compare it to what or who? Once we've decided what we want to look like, then we seek to find the regiment that'll get us there. We go for it, counting calories, exercising, changing our eating habits and glorifying our results. Nice!

But how concern are we about the look of our spiritual bodies? Does our heart need daily cleaning? Does our words bring forth life? Are we picking up books to gain more knowledge throughout the day? Are we defeating from bad habits, associates and new? Let's examine both bodies.

DAY 119

The Karma Café. Serve like the leader you are. Respect another's boundaries as you desire yours to be honored. Honesty is a way of life not a temporary choice. Before applying strong punishment, ask yourself if this is déjà vu? Sometimes we forget who, what and where we use to be, but life doesn't. Be mindful how you dish it out—your spoon may get heavy!

Karma brings us back our fruits from the seeds we planted; good or bad. We must practice doing what is right and pleasing so when the time comes to get back that, in which we planted; we'll be pleased.

If we applause for others as they're celebrating because our time will come, and we'll desire the same love in return.

DAY 120

Our faith begins as a seed that's planted. This seed receives ground (our heart), when we speak and act upon it, the seed is activated. Faith needs a vehicle to travel, move and reach its destiny. Every tree was once a seed, time fought through storms, winds and fires until it grew into a tree.

So, plant your seed (Faith), speak life (our positive words) and watch your tree (promise, destiny, purpose and plans) flourish. Remain fruitful even when the circumstances are critical.

DAY 121

We live in a world where insecurity is on the rise. Media is feeding us fear and lies, jobs pay enough for you to show back up tomorrow, you're totally clueless on who or what you are

dating. Our banks are stealing, mates cheating, social media is telling, friends are betraying, families are killing, the ground is shaking and quaking and children are disrespecting.

We must not be moved, stressed, uncertain, fearful or characterized by what is being portrayed. Trust whatever the process. Keep looking up, remain focused, meditate on those things that are positive even, when hit with a negative, rely on the positive outcome.

DAY 122

Sometimes we may feel others attempt to take us for granted or use us but can anyone honestly be taken advantage of? But, if we are doing things from our heart; it is always a good deed, regardless of others ploy. No one can steal from us or our children and not pay a high cost. So, if anyone has wronged you, don't invest energy in them because it's seen, heard and known and we're covered.

Whatever offenses we've encountered from anyone mentally, emotionally, spiritually, financially and physically—expect payment with interest. Keep doing well and right, our records will and do show that we're going to be taken care of and blessed accordingly.

DAY 123

We beat our heads against the wall seeking answers that someone has already embedded within us. Imagine the many libraries that we've not even tapped into yet. The remedies that can keep us healthy that we've ignored but take meds that are killing us. Think of the elders that can shorten our walk of insanity with a quick word of insight. The foolish

relationships that keep us crying and angry countless times when keen knowledge said, "Let it go, they're trouble, you'll cry more than laugh, it's dead weight, you can't change what refuses to change, clean your glasses because you can do better than that, is that all you think you're worth?"

Next time wisdom sits beside you, seek it, apologize for your ignorance and take life changing notes. Don't let another library be buried without checking out the books.

DAY 124

We've entered a place where we're expected to be obedient in the middle of conflict. Continue moving forward, even if it seems as though the enemy is walking to and from seeking someone to kill, steal or destroy. Just push, which means, there's opposition, resistance and many times pitfalls yet we keep moving forward. We may watch, cry, and suffer, when we are angry, confused, lost, discouraged and yet we continue moving forward. Push against a force that is unseen yet very real. Push, with every fiber in your soul.

Push until something happens. If we remain vigilant in our pushing; there will be a change, a move and a declaration that will bring us into a peaceful place and victory.

DAY 125

Chaos may be all around us, but with all the power that's been instilled with us, we can keep our peace. When we begin to compare ourselves to what is or has been spoken everywhere else could leave us feeling as an outcast. Hearing "nobody else is agreeing, looking, doing or hearing that but you then stand alone, regardless you're trusting the spirit within.

The odds may seem against you but based on the team you're on, you've got the only one that matters.

The many times you aren't invited to the reindeer games because you're soul is too bright, it wasn't to exclude you—it's to define you. When you stand for something and with the only one who count, you're the MAJORITY. Whose team are you on? Major League all the way. Don't allow anyone to define your worth based on numbers because you only need one number—VIP.

DAY 126

We must know that every set up is a position for us to rise up, stand up and look up. It reads "a righteous man falls 7 times and shall rise again..." We've got temporary problems with lifetime promises. We fall down— but we get up, right?

We're forever over comers through the power that's invested in us; if we use it. There will and must be times we're put to the test of how much we can take before we manifest our powers. How do we know miracles can happen, if we're unable to either witness it or be it? Sometimes we may feel we're being picked on, when actually we're being influenced or use to bring forth great testimonials. Make it an awesome day and rise.

DAY 127

We've heard "the yoke is easy and the burden is light", right? If it's heavy, then it's not yours to carry and we've not let go of the weight. Famous words "let go" can be one of the hardest tasks to do, why? Control! We feel we must possess control, so letting go would render us from being in control.

Just as deep anger keeps us out of control, until we surrender this anger as a weapon defeated.

Holding on to unnecessary weight keeps us in bondage not those that have placed the yokes on us. Nothing is more valuable than freedom and peace. Today, we release everyone who has offended, abused, mistreated, lied on us, betrayed us, walked away from us or attempted to destroy us so we can be free. Be grudge-free and lose the weight it carries.

DAY 128

Early this morning as I was meditating, I was able to understand that so many times in our lives, we find out later how immature we've been in our decisions. I used to pray "look over my children while I'm gone and keep them covered" until I realized I wasn't in control of their lives. They didn't belong to me; I was just assigned to look after them.

Sometimes, we find out that we have taken on more than what we were supposed to have taken. Our immature choices have caused us some series of misunderstandings. As we mature, we find out how little control we really have over things and allow the Universe to lead us on our journey and it becomes much more peaceful.

DAY 129

It's been created in most of us to see, hear, experience and know the same thing and yet receive totally different conclusions. You can ask 12 people the same thing and get different replies. We're not created as robots; we're spiritual beings with earthly attachments. When given a problem, we are to search within us for a solution. Outside of us will be others that are

searching within themselves and giving us their answer based on what's within them.

Many times, we're not confident with our own views or wisdom. We seek others knowledge to compare or influence our thoughts. Can you trust that whatever has been placed in you has equipped you with internal knowledge to guide you? What do you see that is not always what the majority sees? Be an original and be content with it.

DAY 130

Do unto others… "Do me like you want to be done, Ginny", Wow! Do we really do people the way we want them to do us? Really? Is our 1st concern, love and thought about the other person or ourselves? Do we treat others the way we desire to be treated? Before starting off each day or turning on anything, let's meditate, collect our thoughts and make concise decisions. Find moments to slip off to meet and commune with your Higher Power before doing anything.

I cry when I realize everywhere I look is life; in the trees, birds, sun, the little baby, the vehicle, in the store, through a song, by my children, in pain, sorrow, laughter etc.… What about you? What's your peace in a storm, sugar in the honeycomb, the wind beneath your wings (felt that one), the balm for the healing, the love of your life and how do treat it right? Can you do outside what you desire to done to you inside?

DAY 131

What or who are we training our children for? Is it NFL, College Professors, Law enforcement, parenting, military, activist, Politicians, liars, deceivers, dropouts, gangsters or what-

ever? I remember when my grandson was born, by the time he was 3 months he was aware of a cell phone because it's the thing his mother kept in her hand. He became familiar with what was connected and surrounded her—his atmosphere.

We use to talk, read and speak to our children, building relationship and forming a bond (our voice). Today, whose voices do our children hear? They're placed in front of the TV, listening to music and connected to Wi-Fi to hear any and everything. Whose voice is our children listening to and who's training or grooming them? Now is the time everyone needs to make changes for our youth.

DAY 132

As our seasons change, are we prepared? Many times when our life takes on a change, has a big upset or is faced with unpleasant issues, we become stressed or uneasy. Many things that come our way has already been filtered out and positioned to get us to the next blessing in life.

If we're spending more time with our spirit than the distractions of this world; we could be prepared for some things. Nothing comes by surprise or without purpose. How can we testify about a miracle unless we've been able to experience it? How do we know that we can come from poverty to wealth, sickness to health, jobless to entrepreneurship, being a nobody to a gift?

This comes from walls we hit, those enemies we thought were friends, a doctor's report of doom to being completely healed. No one enjoys the hell experiences but it's the torment that gets us to praise 115-degree weather because we know it's not over. So be encouraged, if we've been sent to it, it'll get us to our greatest place. Remain in tune with your spirit, nothing

is impossible.

DAY 133

Imagine the roller coaster ride, the excitement of going up and yet realizing although it seems a bit slow going up, you know you must come down. Hands easily goes up as we're going up, hands holding on tight coming down. You hold on for life as you race down, heart racing with fear as you move forward to the unknown. All I'm wishing for is, let this ride end and I live. A friend of mine said yesterday, "many times we scream, "Get me off this ride in tears while digging in our pockets for the money to ride again." Insanity. We say, I hate it, this or them but again today we're there waiting for the next high or low. Life hands us lows, we many times chose our weapons of misery but we must see the light, the positive and lesson so that we're not scarred negatively.

Many lows, valleys, hurts, battles and disasters has entered our lives but what needs to come out of our lives should be brighter, better, newer and greater. Let's be determined to turn EVERY negative into a positive. Look for good and you'll find it because the change comes to take us higher; so hands up.

DAY 134

If you're not watching, then nine times out of ten, you are going to be someone's prey. A prey is the one being hunted for appetite fulfillment. The hunter will look for a prey that's appetizing yet not hard to obtain, catch or get. Sound familiar? How many times have we become someone's prey because of our weaknesses—crying from a loss, broken heart, spiritual

separation, confused, alone, suffering with all kinds of weakness?

When we're at our lowest place or state of mind; we are easily sought out as a prey. Can we be identified as a prey today? If so, let's make sure that if the enemy sees and hears us, they also know we're armed. At some point they'll be arrested, discouraged, move on, silenced, hindered and /or destroyed. Refuse to be acknowledged as a prey!

DAY 135

Amazingly, whatever we love to do is usually our passion. Many of us are doing what we don't love. Why? Is it because of convenience, money, circumstances, inheritance, we're unskilled or what? This can cause us to be out of alignment with our purpose, passion and the plans. Time and focus can place us back in position with what we really enjoy doing.

Find your passion, the very thing you love to do and you would do it even without pay or recognition and make that passion outstanding. Our passions will cause others to be moved by our passion when we present it, display it and/or apply it. Let's find ourselves loving what we do.

DAY 136

Every once in a while, we need to reevaluate our circle and perimeter for any changes that may need to adjust. Everyone shouldn't have the same access, position or standard to your life. Limit your space; once you've decided or established that our space has reached the desired capacity; close it. Our ratio may be different in what our limits are but once reached; we should follow through on finalizing.

Make your boundaries clear and remain firm. These actions may not please everyone, but it'll keep our atmosphere clear of toxicity. Seek balance and then balance.

DAY 137

I Can't.

I can't allow others to determine my destiny.

I can't give up because others did.

I can't live beneath my beliefs even when my faith is challenged.

I can't wait on a paycheck—when my Source and Supplier is far bigger.

I can't cry for those that laugh at me—although I can laugh with those who know how to love me.

I CAN do all things when I know I'm created to overcome all obstacles and can't be stopped unless I stop.

DAY 138

How many people have brought into our life to help us identify who we are? Strangers can walk up to us and begin speaking missing pieces to our lives. There have been countless people who introduced me to me, how about you? They've helped us see who and what we are.

The elderly lady who lived down the road, when I was three (3), who would give me a quarter to see me wiggle (I thought I was dancing). How about the ones that invested in us, pulled love from us and saw the fight in us? Yes, even those who inspired us at a very early age that we searched out once we became grown and found to thank them for making it possible for us to be standing in position today. Even those

that hated and betrayed has a purpose in our lives to teach us.

So, salute to all those that played a part in our living; thank you.

DAY 139

When someone tells us something, it's left to our discretion to believe it or not. But when we KNOW something, nobody has to believe us because it's our truth, solid foundation and guidance.

We've been taught by a lot of people and told a many of things but sometimes we had to learn to remove from our data base other's words and find pure truth.

We sometimes were taught wrong, showed lies and walked in staggering darkness until the LIGHT came. And once you've seen the light, know its truth, darkness is the prisoner and we're free. Let's continue seeking, loving and making positive steps to the wonders of life. Remain in peace.

DAY 140

Remember our urgency isn't another's emergency. Because we're in a panic, stressed or indecisive; our world doesn't pause for us. When we miss a beat, opportunity or moment; that's now a past thought; push forward. Many missed appointments have been designated for greater destinies.

Yesterday, we're on the ropes taking blows from all angles. Today, we wear the belt! Don't be discourage because it looks lost or unbearable; endure as the powerhouse we are and the outcome will be insurmountable. Don't throw in towel, ring the bell or give in; the fight is fixed, and we got this. This isn't an emergency or urgency; it's a war and we answer without

hesitation because we're built for this.

DAY 141

Trust! Trust in whom? Whenever we say we trust, we must look at all areas before making ourselves vulnerable to anyone. Do we truly know that everything we give to out is being shaped, covered, changed, arranged, anointed and released into the atmosphere? Do you believe in is our greatest security system? Whatever you give out in the right heart, we'll be blessed with much more.

Give out your smallest mustard seed faith, and then trust it to grow into a tree of life. Whatever is filtered through the Universe has got to be good when it returns. When you can't see the move, trust the process. No one can be trusted until you know they have and do love you, Trust that!

DAY 142

Ever think about the things you do or say at the wrong time to the wrong person for the wrong reason? What if you could only practice saying the right things and doing the right thing for and to the right people for the right reasons? The pains of the hurt we can cause in someone's life because we don't think before we do or say the things. What if the secrets from our pillows could share its years of tears? How about the heart that continues to mend time and time again and the mind that collects the pieces?

Sometimes we are riding rollercoaster rides of chaos, craziness, drama and heartless invites, and all we need to do is get off the ride and refuse the next invite. Refuse to settle and wait!!!

DAY 143

Ever met someone who would be completely dishonest, unfair, irresponsible, immature and lost yet got others backing them up? It's like watching someone stand outside in a thunderstorm under a tree cursing out the Creator and beside them is that person screaming, "Say it again." Or someone recording another person committing a horrendous act, who's worse the one committing it or the one taking joy in filming it? Don't admire a fool or you will be look upon as foolish. If you see a fool digging a grave for them, don't grab a shovel and dig yours too; move.

DAY 144

We need to read to stimulate our minds. Show me a person that enjoys reading and I can show you someone who reaches endless possibilities. There have been times when we would challenge ourselves to read a book a month. This was difficult for those who hated to read, but easy for those who enjoyed reading. Exercising our mind to be filled daily with something new, gainful, refreshing, touching, educating, resourceful, life changing, inspirational, powerful and obtaining.

Any book has the ability to bring understanding to those who study it and seek guidance and revelation about its contents. How many times have we read something with no comprehension? If there is no understanding, there is no power. Push yourself to read something daily as you strive to build your body, soul and spirit. Working both will perform awesome results. Seek clarity, wise men do.

DAY 145

Ever feel like you're not connected to those around you until a disruption happens. I remember one thanksgiving we all ate dinner and went in the living room with our phones—everybody had electronic device in their hands so it was silent and no family communication. I watched, chuckled and said, "Let's play scrabble, monopoly or spades but let's mingle". Communication is important. Many times, we're in contact with everyone but the ones we NEED to be in contact with. We'll text each other in the same house instead of talking.

We go to businesses, Doctor's offices and any other place and the cell phone is going off or being used. Communication is vital in relationships; family, friends, workplace, etc. yet how we communicate is just as important. How many times have your texts been misread, mislead, mistaken or just missed, when a simple live conversation would have sufficed? Sometimes miss someone enough to talk to them face to face or at least by conversation without the electronic device doing it for you.

DAY 146

We should be always learning because everyone is a teacher. It says, "We're forever learning but never coming to the full knowledge of the truth". We are forever learning unless you have chosen to pause on being foolish. You don't have to be a college graduate to be a teacher—a baby will teach if you're willing to learn. Trees, nature, animals, history and whatever we choose to learn from, will teach us. Pay attention to everyone who crosses your path. They are teachers—good, bad, reckless, immature, liars, thieves, honest, beautiful, valuable, ignorant, forgiven, forgetful, gracious etc. The bad breakup

taught you, the tearful movie taught you, the book, customer service, paychecks, friends, enemies, social sites, they're teaching us. Are we learning? If we are repeating the same things with the expectation of different outcomes, we've not learned we're experimenting and there's a difference. It's difficult to move from lesson to lesson if no knowledge is being obtained, absorbed and processed. Before you see yourself as a great teacher, learn the lessons it could prevent pain, failure, disappointment or bring joy, real love, truth etc. Who's ready for class—knowledge is powerful, the ability to learn is key.

DAY 147

There's a slim chance you'll get the loan, make it through school, recover from an illness, see them again, win in court, give birth, find a real woman/man, become a true success, win an award, publish a best seller, meet destiny on the first try, own a fortune 500 company, see your name in the lights of Hollywood etc. It's slim but possible. When they say it's slim or no chance; choose the slim.

When we're a powerhouse and a force to be reckoned with by ourselves; we can take the slim out of the equation. Send the words into the Cosmos and note the exchange that'll bring us closer to our destination. There are no odds, we can do the impossible on slim; not none.

DAY 148

The day will come that you find out that your insiders are really you outsiders. Remember that there are some people that walk into our lives to connect to our energy, lifestyles, connections, secrets and power sources. Once we've

been awakened to their plot, deceit and plan; we must quickly close the gate, shut the door and pull the line so that we're not drained, destroyed or damaged any further.

Some say make a fool out once; shame of you. I say make a food of me twice; clean your mirror. Every blow that has hit you has identified your power to stand, overcome, endure, suffer and WIN. WE'RE AWESOME LIKE THAT!

DAY 149

Work to get out of the pressure that suffocates you. Sometimes we begin to complain about our splinters and realize that that are those in critical condition. If we're in touch with our surroundings and have the gift of compassion, we'll seek to help those needing us most. While one wants money to buy a meal, another seeks shelter from harm and still another is battling terminal illnesses.

Because someone is smiling at us doesn't mean they're not suffering within. Homeless people are greeting us at the front line with smiles, abused and scared people are giving us soft answers and patience and those most stressed are creating an atmosphere of love. So, know that there are those less fortunate than us that still knows how to bear under and serve us with love and a smile. Take notice of our moment to complain and think about those around us who needs our comfort, love and peace; then serve that.

DAY 150

"That you also aspire to lead a quiet life, to mind your own business, and to work with your own hands as we command you."

Have we ever considered studying to be quiet? Why? How many times have you wished you didn't say what you said? The poison that can flow from our minds onto our tongues; cannot be erased once it is released so be careful.

Let's study to be quiet, listen more, talk less, evaluate, make sure the information is correct and then wait. Everything we know is not for us to tell, some things are just for us to know for future reference. Words do hurt us more than sticks and stones.

DAY 151

Have you noticed that you got some serious haters watching you? Do you know how long they've been there? Your birth wasn't supposed to happen because the enemy knew your mission was pronounced before you were conceived. That's right, the word went out that there would be a YOU, who would change the order of things, minds and the hearts of the people—that you would be an anointed vessel.

Catch this—you're the secret weapon pronounced to this earth and they know it but fight to make sure it remains a secret—even to you. They must kill the dreamer, the mighty warrior, the healer, the strong tower, the royal priesthood, the lily in this valley, the song writer, dancer, author, entrepreneur, the producer, interceder, giant slayer, King, Queen, life speaker etc. Refuse to go under!

DAY 152

Our lives were predestined, it didn't just happen—it was in the plan; the good, indifferent and the bad. We were predestined to be a drug addict, alcoholic, fighter, mentally im-

balanced, intelligent, victim, criminal, mother, father, teacher, healer, strong, weak, leader, follower etc. Without the bad, how could we truly appreciate and be a testimonial of the good. Both good and evil has to be present and though a hard pill to swallow, it's the truth? How would we know what good is if we never experienced bad?

We may have to take side roads. Valleys, mountains, oceans, prisons, sicknesses, curses, abandonment, issues, struggles, anointing, appointments, drugs, pains, sufferings, wilderness, palaces, friendships, enemies, fire, joy etc. We have been called; we don't have to agree with the decision but trust the process.

DAY 153

There's a translation that says this, "Spiritual people comprehend everything, but they themselves aren't understood by anyone. Wow! Spiritual people will understand everything but will never be understood by anyone. If we allow the spirit to lead and guide us, speak for us, so then those who seek to harm us, set us up, or make a mess of our lives will know they have mistaken us. We're not weak, confused, lost, defeated or going the wrong way; our spirit knows everything; all we need to do is obey our spirit. Unless you're on the same road, seeking the same things, and striving to get to the same place—you can't understand me, enjoy me, have peace with me, love me, work with me, stand by me, nor fight with me. You can't understand my flow, anointing, power, vision, purpose or choices unless our spirits are aligned. You are not meant to be understood—but to understand! Just try to birth that today in your life, mind, soul and heart—and only then will the plan for your life open up.

DAY 154

What's your assignment? Most people have no idea, so that keeps them busy in everything but their assignment, which is wasted time and energy. Just as in school, most assignments aren't easy or pleasing but if we carry them out the reward will be grand. I've found some assignments to be very challenging and discouraging and much as I wanted it to be complete; it seems like it would linger on and on. These are usually the people assignments; those that are hard to love, understand or desire to be in their company. I would ask "why do I always get the hard ones?"

Have you ever had someone that didn't know love nor love themselves, yet it was your assignment to teach them what love is through actions not words? This takes a lot of time, patience, possible tears but if we endure until the assignment is complete. When our assignment is done, there's a release and moment of enrichment that will let us know it is finished.

DAY 155

Every day, we live a life that we can't always see our good coming back to us. Reaping is an order made by the Universe, when we do right—right comes back and when we do wrong—wrong comes back. Planting a seed is what we do all the time, consciously or unconscious, with our word, deeds and lifestyle so, we must expect to receive a harvest from that which we planted.

It may take some time before we can see our good coming back but just know it's coming with interest. We must believe that whatever we send out will return with the increase; good or bad. So, let's focus on doing good and being our best despite where, who, what or how because eventually our return

shall come.

DAY 156

How many people have hoped, sweated and dreamed as they placed their last on the chance of being a winner? You don't have to raise your hand—you know we can get caught up in a system of chances instead of trusting what's stable. People will gamble with anything—relationships, jobs, homes, bills, life etc. They will cross their fingers, grit their teeth and silence the world around them hoping... What if? What if you took your house payment and chanced it on hopes of winning? What about those that will slip out on their loved one—in hopes that they will never be caught? Or those who take that hit on the pipe? Call in sick so that you can make the event? AND YOU LOSE!!! Was it worth it?

I love having both feet on the ground and a nest egg in the bank, family worth, people that possess integrity and having a sure backs me up. Who's betting, if we do what's right, we'll win? We possess keys to wealth, we're children of the Kingdom, Royal Priesthood, Blessed, full of favor and chosen—no chances of this being lost.

DAY 157

There is a seed in every seed. Every seed has been designated to bring forth fruit. All fruit was and is expected to be good for something. Are we fruitful? Everything has a season and purpose; everything—birds, trees, insects, fish, people, angels, etc. Why didn't this last? What happened to that? I never thought I would see this! So, glad I was a part of that! In everything, we are expected and instructed to be fruitful

not fruitless.

When we can take nothing and design, fulfill, reshape, embrace, reveal, increase, deliver, possess and declare something. In all of us is the ability to bring forth fruit when we're connected to the root. Production is expected and through obedience; it's accomplished. We're producing life or death, truth or lies, unity or division, love or hate, prosperity or property. Every tree is known by the fruit it bears or bares.

DAY 158

Just when we feel we have finally got things together and we can see clearly, we are blindsided. No matter how we feel things should be—only the divine plans of will prevail. We're repeatedly reminded that our ways are not always the ultimate plan. We must dance to our drumbeat and then we must follow the plans that were created and designed for just us. When we've finally saved enough money, went on enough dates, cried enough times, heard enough lies, made enough vows, broke enough promises, lost enough battles, took enough abuse, said enough hurt, begged enough mercy, hid enough grace, desired enough love, escaped enough hate and finally we're in control.

Then within seconds, it crashes, it dies, it's gone, it's a ghost, it's a lie, it's stolen, it's debt, it's a habit, it's a trick, it's mind blowing, it's betrayal, it's lost, it's a circle; IT'S THE PLANS! We don't have to understand, agree, stand with, vote of speak because it will be done—and it'll absolutely work out for our good because it's the plan.

DAY 159

How do you know how blessed you are? Sometimes it's not until we've lost it all, stricken with a near death experience and talked about by those who we thought to be close. It's during these times we couldn't understand, receive, respect, cherish or testify on being truly blessed because of the hits we're taking. When we've been lied to, forsaken, talked about, persecuted, abused, taken before the courts, drugged through the mud, attacked, betrayed, deserted, mocked, denied, beaten, cheated, or cheated on, whipped, and the list goes on; take notes. Until you've experienced or are experiencing the hardships, disappointments, ridicules and struggles of life, you are truly someone waiting to be blessed to come out. The next time you hear someone say the cliché "I'm blessed and highly favored" ask within—are you really? Today, we desire the glory not the story. Being better than blessed is truly a story or hurts, destructions, sicknesses, persecutions etc. Do you want to be blessed like that?

DAY 160

How many of us realize our biggest problems in life are ourselves? Though it's far easier to blame others for our failures, losses, relationships, decisions, stress, hurts and disappointments; we must admit we are greatest enemy. If we learn to look inside before pointing outside, we would find our biggest enemy within. D. L. Moody says he has more trouble with himself than others and so do we. Yet, we know we feel far better if we are able to blame someone else than the enemy within. What happened? Them! Who did it? Him! Where did it start? Her! Why did you quit? Everybody! Hmm. sounds familiar?

If only we will take responsibility and be accountable for our own choices, mishaps, wrong doings and self-destructive behaviors. As we face our giant in the mirror—we can stand firm and win. Reflection can be troublesome. Trouble don't last always even those we bring about ourselves.

DAY 161

Many of us have played the game— "when I get big I'm going to have ...! How many of us have conquered our dreams and how many are still sleeping? To dream big is to know inside of us is a seed of awesome potential that's more than able to get the job done. To see what really lies within us is totally ridiculous to most, but powerful to the remnant. When we can see a King in an abandoned boy—a Ruler in a dreamer—a Deliverer in a murderer—a Queen in a castaway—an Leader in a silent whisperer—a Writer in a blind man—an example from the child—a Mother in the barren—a Mission through our enemies—a purpose for the accuser—and favor for those who embrace change.

Are you awake so you can work on your dream or are you too busy sleeping through your dream? One of the greatest speeches is "I Have a Dream." We should have a dream so big that we need others to help complete it—I do!

DAY 162

King Solomon was the wisest King that ever lived; so we have been told. His weakness was also his strength—wisdom. For many years, I had believed women were his weakness, but today I see another revelation. The search for wisdom is a journey that never seems to end. Yesterday, I had a long-time

friend come by and said something to me that opened my understanding to wisdom. This revelation may help others. Have you ever found yourself in search for wisdom and trying to absorb all you can from anyone you can? Then you find that there is no more information to receive and no one is even able to penetrate your mind. You continue to search on for more insight, intellect, power, information and wisdom to thrive on. Solomon may have become bored with mediocrity of the simple and kept searching and emptying the minds of those connected. Sometimes we don't know what we're seeking, we just know you long for answers. Often criticized, misunderstood, victimized seeking to find. Many may capture your body and parts of your heart but few impress the mind or can penetrate your intellect. This old friend said, "Many will travel on this road that becomes so lonely because rarely will you find a true conversation on your level." So true, we can be in a full room yet alone. Today, we can be full of wisdom and in search of kindred.

DAY 163

We receive invitations all the time to various places, events and lives yet we make conscious decisions if we'll go or not. Some invites we just need to ignore, block or terminate. These are invitations to pity parties, gossip, ignorance, lies, violence, petty disputes, troublemakers, poverty, back stabbers celebrations, sin etc. Choose not to be connected or involved with invites that kill and don't fulfill. There are many invites but how many of us answer?

Many of us have been called to feast with the right people but feel it's the wrong time or come and don't participate. Everyday there's invitations going out and we must make the choice to go or not. As the world calls us and sends out their invites, are we the chosen few to go or come?

DAY 164

Sometimes we have an early dismissal day; it is when we must allow everything and everyone to be excused from our lives. We cannot be offended nor be consumed by anyone that seeks to release negative energy in our lives. Embrace early dismissals and don't take them personal; they were only meant to get us out before we got locked in. In many cases we want to be rejected early in a relationship before we spend time, money and secrets with someone that wouldn't value them.

If and when we are connected to anyone and are a blessing to them—beware when the time is up, and you become unbearable and dismissed. When someone dismisses us, don't get angry; in time, we'll see why and understand that it wasn't to hurt us but to bless us. Reasons, seasons, and lifetime are the purpose for each person in our lives. Stop allowing people to believe they're that important to your growth, destiny, purpose, vision, journey and overflow. You don't have to cry another tear, write another plea, fight another battle, break another vow, breathe another lie –just allow the early dismissal to take place.

DAY 165

If we are praising instead of grumbling, seeking instead of running, turning instead of continuing—becoming humble instead of prideful—we can expect the healing of our nation instead of destruction of ourselves. We must put our best in the front to attack anything to seek to tear down what we

stand on.

Whenever we're approached by any bad or negative person or thing, we must counterattack it with positive vibes. There's always someone who wants to take us down but we're able to maintain our position and stand and find the good in any bad situation. For we know that there's nothing permanent.

DAY 166

How many times have our hearts gotten us in the most trouble? Our emotions are ridiculous at times. You say I'm not going to ever do, be or say that and one day—oops! The heart that we really need to feed is our soul and mind. We say that we love with our whole heart and then down the road—evil and hatred flows out. The heart can be very wicked—just get mad and watch the things that can pour out of it. We're giving and taking back our hearts to so many people, because we do not fully understand it or its magnitude.

Let's guard our hearts—everyone and everything shouldn't have access to our trusting heart. Our hearts should be treated with great care, protected from that which desires to harm and/or crush it. When we choose or decide to share or reveal our hearts; we should've already tested the ground for pure love. Be mindful of whose presence we want to reveal our heart to and why because everyone isn't worthy for that privilege. Have a heart-felt lovely day.

DAY 167

There's something so beautiful about the rain; its sound, its smell and its beauty. This has the same affect in the spiritual realm when we ask to be rained upon. Showers of bless-

ings begin to flow yet the after effects may not be what we desire. Ever ask for peace and hell knocks on the door? — Desired love and had to battle with hate—sought joy and anger arose—prayed for a friend and found an enemy. You know it's when you seek to touch someone else's life and yours go under fire. I remember interceding over someone's house and marriage and mine fall apart!

We must understand that when we're asking for rain, we might have to deal with the mud, floods, and storms—because it comes with the rain. Rain is so beautiful, and its purpose is more majestic than we know; so let it pour down on me, I am so ready.

DAY 168

I have a sister who enjoys rainbow sightings because it makes her think of the promises. We can think of some promises that we've been given; some that were held, and others broken but still all promises. I would listen to children asking their parents to promise them this or another, which meant to me that there were many times they had been disappointed by their words. A promise isn't meant to be taken or given lightly; it is a keepsake, it's a bond and it's a vow. There have been personal promises I have been given to hold on to that hasn't surfaced but I still believe shall come.

I was never told that I would not be tempted to lie, cheat, fall away, be discouraged, be attacked by sickness, divorce, broken hearted, lose at love or even lose a loved one. Nor was I told that I would never have enemies, become displaced, etc.—but I could promise myself that I'll live to conquer. The rainbow is filled with so many colors that stretch from Alpha to Omega (our beginning to our end). You can see the rain-

bow, but you can't touch its glory. When we see the majestic rainbow—remember every promise that's been made to you.

DAY 169

When I think about a wave, I see resistance and its ability to do different. When the water wants to remain calm, the wave resists. Yet within its resistance brings life. It causes the ocean, sea, beach or springs to fulfill the plans of life in its very breathing. It's inhaling and exhaling—its life is beautified by its majestic purpose. Many of us like to remain calm, comfortable and cause small ripples. I choose to be a wave, defiant to the norm—fighting for a cause, affecting those within, daring to be different and not ashamed—knowing that beauty is always in the eyes of the beholder not the confined.

Let's dare to step out into the unknown, unreal, become scorned, a trailblazer—one who would defy gravity, the one, unique without feelings of how others may see or perceive us. Encourage the children to make waves—anyone can cause a ripple. Waves are tried, admired, talked about, challenged, peculiar, unique every time, breathtaking and carefully designed with no limits. Sounds awesome to me! Try making waves sometime—you just might like it.

DAY 170

Every time we are attacked, there's a negative power that attempts to consume us. Many begin to give up by giving in. Yet, throughout the Universe, enemies were always planted, involved, appearing and speaking into our lives. The enemy will rise up in our Heaven and attempt to turn it upside down. Our enemy wants so much recognition and will gather

a crew to back them in the attempt to destroy us. We'll call it mutiny. That's when a person doesn't agree with you but instead of moving on—they whisper into the ears of others for support. Our enemy(ies) will use anything—sickness, poverty, emotions, media and anyone—family, friends, foes, mates, businesses, customer service, doctors, teachers and anywhere—home, work, grocery stores, vacations, churches, hospitals, and highways to start a war. We've all been attacked, have attacked and understand attacks of our minds, heart, life, business, livelihood, finances, character etc. today let's stand on our peace and hold its position.

DAY 171

Many people go through stages in their life where they desire to be like someone else—perhaps they just want to look like what is trending. We take what we start with as human beings and attempt to transform ourselves—change. I marvel at the butterfly that once crawled on the ground. It could easily have been stepped upon in its caterpillar state. The caterpillar now transformed into a butterfly has wings and can fly—lessening the chances of being crushed under someone's foot.

Anyone can mimic what they see. Yet to be exceptional, refusing to remain status quo—take great courage. As the caterpillar that no longer desire to crawl but to fly—to feel the air of freedom on your wings instead of the dirt on your feet. How many of us can feel the transformations happening in our lives right now? Know as you begin your journey; everyone isn't going to be happy for you because they'll know you won't be mediocre anymore. Expect resistance but don't stop; transform.

DAY 172

Can we trust what we are unable to see? That's the question many try to throw at me. Of course, we do it every day. We go to work trusting we'll get paid on their payday. We trust our cars to take us from A to B. We trust our homes to shelter us, our children to love us—our spouses to cover us, our hearts to direct us, our minds to steady us, our bodies to carry us and yet within each of these resources there's no guarantee. Why? Because we don't know if any of these things can be trusted nor its true capability yet we trust it.

We believe in many things that we can't see. Our heart is one, we feel its beat and KNOW it's there but we can't see it. We read about its purpose and yet we somehow can get the heart to not only just beat but to love. That center object in our chest is known to love—Wow! How? Sometimes we seek out only what looks like us to trust—that's not the heart, that's the mind.

DAY 173

Time for a bit of history! Someone said, let's take this piece of charcoal that stressed itself clean and make it priceless. We buy whatever we hear is a big seller. Name brand shoes, bags, clothes, perfumes and then convince ourselves we're in the NEW when technically you're recycling the old. Who does that? Billionaires don't. If we want to be always scratching the surface, keep spending from the bottom. Women were taught—the bigger the diamond—the greater the value; really?

Imagine how many best seller tactics we've brought because someone said so and yet the item was valueless—wasting precious assets on liabilities. When we want to be prosperous,

we'll stop investing in what people say and begin believing in our own success story. Sadly, many will sleep, refusing to believe or awaken to truth because the lie always looks better. If we could truly count up the cost on how much we've spent off someone's word, it would speak volumes. Let him or her who has an ear—hear. What is insanity again? Doing the same thing over and over and expecting different results. We need to be always available to know History; and then we just need to be teachable and reachable.

DAY 174

Hiccups

Hiccup – a temporary or minor difficulty or setback. "Just a little hiccup in our usually wonderful service" Now that we've defined it, can we locate it or them? Minor setbacks—hiccup. Bad relationship—hiccup. Wrong decision—hiccup. We've all had or have them but realizing they are only temporary though uncomfortable. Whatever storm, trial, pain or mishap we may be facing, see it as a hiccup. It may come at the worse time, bring you embarrassment, cause pain or last way top long, still—it is a hiccup. The sooner you identify the hiccup—the sooner you can apply the cure. In our lives, we have all experience hiccups. As we mature—we master them.

My brother plays tennis so well-- he masters the court. If I attempt to get on the court with him, there is no question who would dominate. When he first began to play tennis—he didn't know the court—time made him a master player—along with wisdom and repetitive training. We'll never master anything hitting and missing. It takes persistence, dedication and true relationship to be on the winning team against hiccups.

DAY 175

Ve-hi-cle

Noun

A thing used for transporting people or goods, especially on land, such as a car truck, or cart.

Synonyms: means of transport, conveyance, motor vehicle "a stolen vehicle"

A thing used to express, embody, or fulfill something.

"I use paint as a vehicle for my ideas"

Synonyms: channel, medium, conduit, means, means of expression, agency, agent, instrument, mechanism, organ, apparatus

"a vehicle for the communication of original ideas"

Everyone acts as some kind of vehicle, transporting, delivering, bringing, taking or expressing something or someone.

People will bring or convey information, issues, trouble, love, forgiveness, loyalty, patience, confusion, magic, miracles, salvation, joy, peace, torment and the list goes on. We pack our vehicles every day, whether big or small, compact or trucks, boats, planes or trains, we have the ability to move or hinder time, people, opportunities, or life. Someone is being used to deliver you something—think before you unload anything. Through many travels, we learn to adapt, convert, transport or deny life's lessons. Pick your vehicle, travel your path and transport the blessings to everyone you meet.

DAY 176

Amazing! Someone is surprised that we are still here—on top, happy, healed, delivered, set free, married, prospering, building network, traveling, making it without them, found ourselves, encouraged, still praying, changed our number, ad-

dress and position. Surprise! Go ahead and surprise someone every day in how great we really are. Let's not be afraid to lose dead weight, tell an enemy—no thank you, head for the moon, build our own castle, make liars out of monsters and trust the process no matter what. Surprise! —we're making it when the odds are against us. That's when we keep being blessed with the SURPRISES! Keep waiting for another one.

DAY 177

Seasons do change and when it does, we must adapt. We're always going through seasons but are we changing with them? Timing is so important in our lives. Too many times we miss opportunities, people, businesses, ministry, blessings, friends, wealth and so much more because we miss our timing.

Think about the many times you should have moved later, but wanted it now or was supposed to go after it now but waited. How to recognize the season we are in is to sharpen our sensitivity to the spirit—listen to the guidance and finally be obedient. Let's do a test—what season are you in now and are you obedient in it?

DAY 178

Some excuses can become bad habits. We can have an excuse for any and everything we don't want to do. One of the greatest excuses is "I don't or didn't have time." This excuse is used most the time—correct? It is better to have said, "I didn't take the time to do it." Most of us have or had the time; we just don't use our time wisely. Think about the time hours that we spend watching TV, playing games, monitoring social media etc. We find time to do what we truly want to do and

find excuses for not doing, going, saying, or being what we don't desire.

Some excuses can become decorated lies, which can make habitual liars, ouch. Sometimes the best way to break a bad habit is to not start one. The next time we are about to make an excuse, let's make sure it's not a lie. Turn your "I can't into "I'll try."

DAY 179

Though the visions tarry, yet I will wait on it. A vision is to be able to see and not to just see but to understand what you're seeing. An example; you look at the sale paper and see something you want or need, you then can see yourself having it. So, you begin your journey so that you are able to receive and possess it. The sale can show you a vision that you activated by preparing yourself to go after it. There's time between when you saw it and when you got it—yet you proceeded until you succeeded.

We should always be ready for a powerful vision. We should always see where we desire to go and nothing and no one can block or stop us. Proceed after your vision until you've succeeded. There's no true delay when you deny time access to the vision. Everyone can't, won't, and don't see your vision because it wasn't given to them—it's yours. Trust that and keep it moving. Stop wasting time explaining a vision to someone who refuses to understand your destiny.

DAY 180

It's a known fact that people will spread bad news faster than good news. Even if it began as good news, they could

make it bad. Your friend gets a new car—good news, right? Sure until they add the gossip— "you know they can't afford it,--let's see how long they keep it,--they paid too much for it and I heard that type of car is not a good car!" Sound familiar?

Annie's pregnant. Good new, right? Until you hear gossip like, "How many is that, they're barely able to keep the other one, don't they believe in birth control?" Peggy and Rob got married—good news until you hear, "It's about time, how many marriages does this make? They are crazy and broke now. Good news is the definition of the pleasant truth; even then, there's shade. Rev Harris is having a revival next week—good news, until—Must need money again, how many members they got, I'm not going cuz they got a lot of mess in there.

We must work on celebrating someone else's good news without killing it without adding negative talk to it. Let's practice keeping good news—good news and killing the spread of bad news. You'll never please everybody so focus on pleasing yourself and changing ourselves can make changes around us.

DAY 181

Why is it that we can always see outside the glass but NEVER into the glass? Isn't the glass the same looing out as it is looking in? So, when we can see other's problems, issues, mistakes, imperfections and struggles, remember we too may have the same challenges. There's a reflection in our mirror we need to be examining more than who's outside of the glass.

I love to reflect and see the things that have been accomplished, still needs work and those things I'm still unveiling. Reflecting allows us to look at where we are and how or why we got here; plus to have directives where we plan on going next. Inhale and observe inside the looking glass instead of

outside the window.

DAY 182

Ever try to hold your breath to button? Or try to attempt to squeeze a size 10 into an 8 or a 38 waist into a 34 waist? Or park a large tractor in a bike lane? They all sound ridiculous but how many times we try to fit in places we know we've outgrown, found to be toxic or continuously negative.

Why remain in a place, position or relationship that brings pain instead of joy, can cause tears instead of laughter and in torment instead of peace? Our answer is to become fit or quit, choose to become more fit in whatever place or time, we're in.

DAY 183

When the worse, most hurtful or unexpected blow makes your heart hurt—mind spin, body buckle, remember it's not what you are served—it's what you do with it. The more sour the lemons, the sweeter the lemonade. Don't allow lemons to define your next move, stage, relationship or destiny—you bring the sugar, your love, your strength and your power.

Make sure we're able to have the final say; however, way they may choose to input. We have been equipped for everything, everyone and everywhere and every lemon will introduce us closer to the plan. Let's make our best and sweetest lemonade whenever we're given lemons.

DAY 184

I chose to live in a gated community, where everyone doesn't have access to me or my livelihood. When someone says to me, I didn't know you moved; it's becuz they don't have access to my life. When I get calls or texts asking me how I'm doing and my response is "Absolutely wonderful", it doesn't matter if I'm in ICU with tubes in my stomach and throat. If they don't have privy to my life, my response is absolutely wonderful.

I'm very careful who comes in my close proximity and the number is usually less than 7. My pains, hurts, gains, loss or triumphs are gated. Family, friends or foes are all aware of the gated

DAY 185

Every day, we're in a battle to remain in peace while our spirit fights our battles. Media many times alerts us to fear. This fear causes us many times to become its victims. We must be reassured that we have nothing to us to fear. We have not been given the power of fear—weapons will come, battles are created, hatred surrounds us, lies overwhelm us and a storm is coming BUT NO Weapon formed against us—you or me, will PROSPER.

We are empowered to cancel the assignments of our enemies—sickness, disease, mental disorders, poverty, death, destruction and my curse thing. We must use our weapons of love, power, truth, life and faith to block every evil thought, plot, person, place or thing that comes against us. This is not the time to retreat; but to stand and believe that we shall conquer all fear and trust our purpose while on this journey.

DAY 186

The beginning of wisdom sometimes is in just the asking.

There is an answer to every problem. Many times, we just haven't asked. Ask who, we may be asking? Whoever is available to give the right and truthful answer that will be clothed with wisdom. Have you ever looked at someone and know that we possess the answer to their problem, yet they don't desire to now it? Imagine how many have looked at our problems and possessed the answers, yet we're not seeking them out. Asking sometimes may simply mean we realize that doing it our way isn't working.

Never feel we know it all, while drowning in your own misery and frustration. Many of us refuse to ask, seek help or knock on doors. Pride normally leaves us in the same condition, with the same people, doing the same thing that's not working. Wisdom will get us out of those ruts and finding solutions to some really needed circumstances.

DAY 187

When we know and respect our integrity, it will sometimes make others uncomfortable when we tell them the truth. The truth is capable of standing alone, it needs no defense team, no confirmation; it only needs to be exposed. There are those who believe they've covered up the truth, denied the truth and even swore against the truth but the truth can't be hidden. Give truth its platform and door; it'll work silently but successfully in revealing itself.

The truth can make us angry yet it's still the truth. When speaking the truth, it can ignite fires to the point that warrants could be place for its arrest. Whenever we stand on the truth, others around us may not want to be in close proximity of us for fear of identifying their lies. The truth did not build a synagogue, it built a message. Sometimes, it's the message, other

times—it's the messenger that brings us truths that makes us comfortable. Receive it anyway.

DAY 188

How pleasant it is to know that each day gives us new mercy every morning. Last night's worries, fears, disappointments and tears are not welcomed to this morning glory. Whatever happened in this day cannot affect our tomorrows unless we allow it to do us. We create our own world around us and then we are able to mold and make it into what we desire it to be.

Even when troubles come, we're able to maneuver it into the greater, because we've invested in keeping our peace and harmony intact. When we've rose up in a place that we know the importance of our positive energy being charged; we immediately dismiss negative people, energy, remarks and zones. We are capable of making everyday a positive and rewarding day with new mercies and Fabulous outcomes.

DAY 189

Going through the process! We know this can be such a challenge. Process isn't always easy or quick but always necessary. Ever notice how easy it is to get into a mess—but how hard the process is in getting out. The process seems unending. Our parents would harp on the words "trouble is easy to find but hard to get out of,"—yet we felt like we had the monopoly to the maze—only to find someone changed the locks and didn't leave you the key.

Today, wherever we are in life is where we were meant to be.

Trust the process even when you can't understand it, we

don't like it; we fight it, cry about it, misunderstand it or try to ignore it; trust the process. I've sat on the beach and watched this; those that challenged the waves (surfing), those that played in the waves (swimmers), and those that stood at the shore (waders), those that observed the waves (students) and those that simply floated. Each one is going through the process, just differently—however with a purpose. Process is necessary and can be quite timely, costly and painful but trust it because it is the processor. Today, note that one is either preparing to be processed, is processing or has been processed.

DAY 190

We all have developed patterns in our brain that make us think a certain way. This pattern allows us to do the same thing without much thought because the pattern is there. Hmmm. Things we were taught as children, form patterns and we repeat these patterns. Those who were introduced to reading, music, TV, abuse, love etc— process that unique pattern that causes us to repeat without thought. So when someone or something attempts to introduce us to the new, we must learn a new pattern. How? — With repetitive synchronization. Example: in order to learn a new song, we must open our minds to receive new sounds, words and meaning. With this, a new pattern is developed in our brain. We can't imagine the many patterns we have and can still receive.

We must rid ourselves of old, misinformed, wrong, hateful, negative and lying patterns so we can indulge in a newness of mind. When we renew our minds, our bodies, heart and words change because our thought patterns have changed. We can't keep pouring evil thoughts in a new heart—something is going to break. Let's be willing to have new ways by

beginning with new patterns. Myth says, "You can't teach an old dog new tricks". Fact says, "If the dog is willing, all things are possible.

DAY 191

Sometimes we must be quiet and listen because our world always has something to say. Remember everyone is a teacher, if we operate as students who desire and are willing to learn. I can't repeat this enough times; we're being taught daily if we're paying attention. I'm determined to learn something new every day and if I get introduced to much more lessons; I'm ecstatic.

I get excited when I'm able to open books in people lives; if we take the time to sit down and absorb the many lessons; we'll be far more advanced. Our teachers have their own degrees embedded in them through their walks in this life. They've got shortcuts, warnings, successes, businesses information, spiritual guidance and so much more if we would only take the time to choose to read or listen. Some lessons are free, some you'll pay for, and others are just waiting for us to embrace.

DAY 192

So many times, we shake our heads on the final decision we make when the first one was the right one. Sometimes it's the whispers that will be warning us; like—don't say anything, don't go, help them, stand your position, believe etc. Small and soft whispers usually don't get the attention like those loud commands, directives, and forces such as—do it now!, don't let that slide, stand up for yourself, or— go for it!

Practice listening to the whisper; in it can come many

words of wisdom and heartbeats of unity. The only way to hear a whisper is to study to be quite and to keep our tone and volume to a place it's not blocking the whisper. When your life is at peace, the voice of a whisper is stronger than when you are in turmoil. Pay attention to the whisper.

DAY 193

The true power of unity/harmony can tear down walls, turn enemies into friends, heal broken hearts, revive the dead, bring peace in the midst of storms, destroy plots and whatever you need and believe. The key to this powerful component is being open to receive such information and knowledge and the wisdom to use it. It's being able to apply the correct words and allowing the words to have assignments because they'll stir up the spiritual to change the natural.

It's the power of these words that's not shaken by circumstances, moved by numbers, silenced by ignorance, forgotten in history, buried by miracles, stunned by agape love, chased by fear or hindered by doubt. It's this power that summons change, deliverance, love, forgiveness, joy, peace, power etc. True power brings liberty and forever results.

DAY 194

R (are) –U (you) –N (in) season for me? Am I in season 4 you? Very seldom do we cry over our seasons changing—yet how many times have we cried over seasonal people. Seasonal people are those who come in and out of our lives. Very few people are assigned in our lives forever—most are just seasonal. Seasons are temporary. They each serve a purpose and they prepare us for the next one. As badly as we wish we could

contain our favorite season, we know it impossible. Instead of crying of the season's changes—we adjust ourselves. Are you in season for me, is the question we must ask ourselves to every assigned person in our lives. Do we desire to swim in the ocean during the winter cold? If we do—we know that results could be deadly. Why? Because the season for swimming has changed, but we can still admire its splendor. Everyone comes to life to complete an assignment. The assignment that we must complete could last for a brief moment, maybe for days, weeks or years; but few are for a lifetime. Accept the beauty of seasonal encounters, temporary changes and lifetime lessons.

DAY 195

Sometimes you got to stop allowing what's happening around us to hinder our next move. We're always faced with distractions that can cause us to miss our moment, appointment, assignment, location, purpose, vision and connection. It doesn't take much to make us hesitate; become misguided, afraid, lost, unsure, frustrated, and angry or disappointed. A news flash, a picture, text, phone call, bill, letter, bad report, a breakup, break in, break down or break through. Whatever has our attention should be pointing us directly to our destiny, if not, refocus.

The story of the ten spies saw the new life too big, scary and insurmountable. The true two saw the life as awesome, greater, the answer to their promises as obtainable. When your vision is bigger, all your enemies will become smaller. See your debt erased, your health phenomenal, your life untouchable, your love being forever. Always remember, Grace surrounds us, Mercy protects us, Blood covers us, Love becomes us and makes our focus clearer.

DAY 196

We know waiting can be frustrating, painful, and uncomfortable and possibly discouraging yet is a very important part of the process of life. The process of perfection comes through the wait. The blooming of a rose, the beauty and value of the pearl or diamond, the newborn baby, adulthood, friendship, success, anointing and the list continues; all comes from waiting.

What good is the cake that hasn't been fully baked, the spareribs that wasn't grilled, a checking account with no money, a mansion with no one living in it, a world without love? Patience can be bitter or sweet, it depends on who does the pouring. Wait on the promise, you've waited on others and found out the rewards are not the same. When we get tired of waiting, wait a little longer, it'll work beautifully. Promise!

DAY 197

How many times in our lives have we experienced being in or around dry bones? Seeking Life, purpose and love yet surrounded by dry bones. We're called into the abundant life; full of joy, peace, love, faith and so much more yet we find ourselves waking up for days in the valley of dry bones. Lifeless! Existing but not living because we've been consumed by the cares, burdens, hurts and pains of this world. Today, we send a word to our spirits today that says, "Live."

There's been an upset, a sweet touch, divine miracle, ridiculous blessing, a computer error, debt cancellation, unexplainable peace, mighty release, righteous judgment, decreed home, committed marriage, delivered loved one, anointed experience, blood drenching covering, fierce war cry. There have been Life changing blessings, and a breakthrough and

untouchable healing today out of the valley. Enjoy!

DAY 198

How many times have we suffered through situations that we were told not to do? Many of us rather walk the dark side of life than to commit to the light. Anytime we disobey, we miss opportunities, blessings, promotions, relationships, keys and trust. Think of how many doors have stayed shut because we were not ready to be obedient. We desire the best but refuse to submit to the authority, guidance and lifestyle. We can't mix oil (the anointing) with Poison Ivy (the cursed thing) and expect greatness.

Do we need some doors opened? Now, listen to what is speaking, directing, orchestrating, and synchronizing to get us into our blessed place. It may not look like what we thought—smell like what we imagined or positioned where we desired it to be but if we obey—blessings will flow. Obedience is knocking—who's ready to obey and move?

DAY 199

What we eat has so much to do with our health. If we are not putting in the right things to cause a constant flow, we can become constipated. Constipation is toxic buildup. Toxic waste can be deadly. So many times, we are carrying anger, hurt, confusion, ignorance, unforgiving, jealousy, hatred and other unresolved issues that we build up. If there's no release or relief, we're in a very unhealthy position, possibly even deadly.

What we put in us must be healthy to our minds, heart, and body or our souls will pay. If you need to lose weight,

then get rid of the negative attitude, people, habits and intake. Let's take a look at those toxic intakes that we allow to enter into us that constipate our mind and life. Today—we seek release from every deadly thing that has clogged our mind, heart and body from His plans, purpose and promise. We will seek after the good so we can live the abundant life. It we're emotionally, spiritually, or physically toxic—today we turn it all around in so we can be receiving all of the goodness— even during bad serving.

DAY 200

Whether we are pizza lovers, steak fanatic, BBQ grubber or salad topper; always remember that there are truly different strokes for different folks. We don't have to think, act or believe the same things yet our hearts can still be in unison. I've got a sister that loves dark colors and earth tones, I'm into bright and vibrant colors but we blend tighter than anyone could imagine in our hearts. We can be so different yet so intertwined.

We don't have to enjoy the same things, love the same foods, wear the same styles, have the same taste in selecting mates but our hearts are so close. This is being able to accept that there are differences in our lives, but this doesn't need to separate us from our love. Let's learn to embrace others despite differences unless it's harmful to us.

DAY 201

Three things that I value very high is Integrity, Truth and Love. A person who lacks these important qualities is not considered assets to me.

There are times we must put up clear and direct signs to protect these well laid traits. Anyone who tries to challenge, oppose or destroy those things should be left at a distance.

Trust your inner spirit, intuition or whatever name you choose to call it and never allow anyone or anything to make you question it. Trust yourself that your spiritual guidance within is well trained, instructed and powerful enough to be spot on accurate. Without its presence; we're an easy prey, helpless creatures and blind souls, so hold your position, trust you and let the Universe breathe.

DAY 202

Every day is a good day to start something new or let go of something old. As we step into each day, breathe out newness and inhale the changes that are coming in our lives. Take on a project or complete one, pick up a book to increase our knowledge or challenge you to something that was a hard task.

Being self- aware is truly a priceless asset. When we realize that working on ourselves is a full-time responsibility; we'll refrain from focusing on anyone else's shortcomings.

Everyday should be a great day to wake up to a better us, based on the work we've put in yesterday. We own our day, so shower it with all we desire to see in it.

DAY 203

We must know when to use the pin vs. the pen. Sometimes when we're watching someone's life, we may feel it necessary to use a pin because they're not flowing as you. But it may be wiser to use a pen and take notes.

Everybody isn't expected to dance to our beat or under-

stand our moves but what they do with that information could be critical. Let's be mindful, we don't know another person's life based on the chapter we entered. So, the importance of a pen is far better than the pin in most instances.

DAY 204

Today we want to talk about the story of the Sleeping Bear. The bear has the right and is prepared to hibernate. When the bear is in hibernation, and you choose to go into the bear's den then you go under your own risk. Once in the Bear's den, you may choose to take a picture of the bear while it sleeps but it is again at your own risk. The bear is sleeping because he has chosen and needs to hibernate. When it is in its hibernation stages, please leave the bear alone. Once you have intruded on a sleeping bear, you cannot be upset with the bear because it attacks. If the bear awakes because you have troubled the bear and it goes into attack mode, you now know you have trespassed.

This also applies to us that may want to agitate another person's life, for some unforeseen reason. Because a person is usually in a great mood and smiling, we may want to poke or tease them, not knowing what that person is needing to be delivered from. Disturbing that person's peace could be detrimental and cause a negative response. So, if you see someone at peace and minding their own business; let them rest. Today's advice is when the bear is sleeping let it sleep or you could face terrible consequences. Sometimes we're the bear.

DAY 205

Every side road, every detour, every construction site has been strategically place in our lives to get us where we are today. No matter where we are, it was designed for us to be here, right here. Sometimes we are in a rush to get something or get somewhere that we have been delayed from, but we must remain patient. What we feel we need today can truly wait for tomorrow. We have no idea what's before us but if we wait, we will find we've be trained and prepared when it gets here. There's nothing worse than going into something unprepared and with no knowledge. So, wait. Wait and believe that your time has already been selected for you to win.

DAY 206

Today, I would love to express the importance of timing. One of things I've admired is the art and talent of Double Dutch jumping is timing. As a child I mastered jump rope with ease, but Double Dutch made me focus on timing; when to get in and out.

Two ropes, not one moving two different directions yet meeting time. Whoa! Life at its best description reminds me of Double Dutch. You wait for the rhythm of timing to let you know when to get in, and then you must remain on sync while inside the ropes. You're allowed to do turns, flips or anything as long as you don't miss the timing. The ropes can move slow and then speed up, yet our only focus is here and knows the timing. Sometimes someone else jumps in and we must jump out but still we must know the time. Know when to get in, how to stay in no matter the changes and the time to exit. Our life is synced with time, and we must know how to watch, listen and wait then move in time.

DAY 207

Let's not compare our lives to anyone. We cannot be aligned with everyone's expectation of us. When we learn to accept others for who and what they are; we can then focus on own identities. We debate about small things and make it big. Whatever someone else decides to do with their life isn't our project. We should have goals, expectations, visions and plans of own so big; that'll it take up too much of our time to get distracted by things that don't concern us.

What we're building, dreaming, seeing and becoming needs our full attention. Let's not get weary or worried, we're built to be us not anyone else; be absolutely great at it.

DAY 208

Somethings are just what they are! You don't have to explain it, understand it or reveal it; it's just what it is. And we must know that it'll make sense as we move forward.

Don't waste valuable moments on ignorant people. Don't spend what you can't afford to lose and don't reveal your secrets, life or next moves with anybody. Those that truly know, care and love you will flow and vibe with you and the outcome; regardless. At least, we know our power isn't handed to anyone that has master skills in destruction, manipulation and lies nor possess keys to our future.

Silence isn't always golden but could be critically necessary.

DAY 209

Sometimes we just need to clear our minds, detox our lives and make better decisions. What we do know is, most of where we are, who we are and what we possess has transpired by the choices we've made.

When we're desperate, confused, hurt angry or other emotional wreck; we can make some of the worse moves. Like being upset and going shopping to buy stuff we done need with the funds we know is destined for other things. We could choose the wrong partner, location, words or project when we're not focused.

That's the purpose for meditation, which we're supposed to do daily, correct? We need to detox ourselves from unhealthy thoughts, people, foods, habits and decisions. Let's take time to silence everything around us and listen within, you'll be surprised to what we may hear. I, may occasionally ride in my car without music, sit in my room with no distractions or relax on the deck alone and listen for spiritual insight.

DAY 210

How do we know if we can succeed until we try it? Someone thought about inside plumbing, automobile, creating a library, schools, sewing and the list is endless. How many ideas have we've had and sat on, just to watch someone else do it? Our minds are awesome and once we combine our thoughts with actions, there's no limits for us. I'm amazed all the day by someone's ability to master things that at one time was only a seed (thought). Don't waste another day questioning your ideas; use them to bring life all over our Universe. No one can be you, do as you do, is expected to shine as you so go get your dream, take your place and make history.

DAY 211

Do we love people for who they are or what they are? Most are unable to love for both though we can say it. Who a person is, is who they are from birth; their mental, social, physical and spiritual state. What they are is a title we're given, a status we carry or a lifestyle we live.

Example: I love you because you're my mother, but I don't like you as a person or I love you as my friend but not as parent. Who a person is has nothing to with the title before their name. Take away the Dr, Teacher, Mrs., Judge or etc., they're still.... We can always find someone we love as a title but not a person. To completely love a person for whom and what they are is rare though spoken frequently. Reflecting...

DAY 212

When someone tells us something, it's left to discretion to believe it or not. But when we know something, nobody has to believe us because it's our truth, solid foundation and guidance. We've been taught a lot of people and told a many of things but sometimes we have to learn to remove things from our data base and find the truth. Sometimes we were taught wrong, showed lies and walked in staggering darkness until the LIGHT comes. And once we've seen the light, know its truth; darkness is now the prisoner and we're free. Let's continue seeking, loving and making positive steps to the wonders of life. Remain in your peace.

DAY 213

As I rose this morning, I felt my mother's presence and said, "Today's your day, momma". I was going to live this day for my mother, and I began my day as her and spoke great things in the atmosphere. I slowed down my emotions and gave people passes on things I would have addressed.

As my day flowed, I saw things better, felt better and got great returns today. I then realized that every day is a gift and gifts are precious. Unwrap them slowly to enjoy the anticipation of what's inside. As we're about to get to the prize, we can inhale and become thankful that we are receiving and were found worthy to be given whatever we obtain. Call in your peace, love, joy, miracles, healing and directions; then start moving and watching it manifest. If the day looks stormy and rough, we need to see it through the eyes of Faith.

Let's rise up proclaiming and lay down praising. We got the power to move, change, hinder, darken or lift our spirit, atmosphere, mindset, position, perception or etc.

DAY 214

Let's not waste words on deaf ears. If they're not listening to what we're saying, maybe they'll pay attention to what we're doing. We can speak much louder by the words we live than those we talk about. Seek balance; it's such an important key to our prosperous future. Whatever we're desiring or pursuing, it must be illustrated not what we're talking but by what we're accomplishing. The less others know of your intent, the further we may get in succeeding. You can tell one wrong person and be delayed or stopped. Work in silence, sometimes alone and let your work speak for you. Your complete production is your introduction!

DAY 215

It's time to Solar Up! Have you ever realized that we're so Solar? We're so connected to the power source (Sun) and when it moves; we're capable on remaining charged. The power that's invested in us is meant to hold us when things get dark and uncertain. If our storms come and we've not been receiving our strength of power, we won't survive. So Solar up and maintain the power (charge) becuz we're going to need it. And remember our power isn't solitary; we can maintain, charge and give power to others. We can be available for those weaken, injured, broken and out of sync, to build a charge. But be selective becuz our solar might not be able to hold or connect to everything. Wisdom needed.

DAY 216

Never allow anyone to be comfortable in trying you poison you. Whether it's a toxic relationship, workplace, environment, food or person; protect yourself.

Anything toxic is a poison that can slowly or quickly kill, steal or destroy our lives. Yet, it seems we know that it's not good for us, but it can be good to us.

We're always told that this food, drink, place or person isn't good for us and is very unhealthy yet, we want it. I've tried breaking toxic stuff (sodas*Pepsi), meats, TV and the list goes on. But the desire to have it is greater than the desire to go without out; unfortunately.

We know its toxic (poisoning our being) yet we're engaging in it. Why?

DAY 217

Have you ever meant someone that lied so much that they forgot it was a lie? One of few people I'm not fond of; is a liar.

They're forever trying to convince us to trust them, with a lie. We can tell a lie, live a lie or project a lie; they're all the same to me.

The truth not only sets us free, it brings us freedom and helps us to seek it out. The truth will bring light on any dark area, situation or person.

I'll always repeat" hurt me with the truth, don't kiss me with a lie". Decide today if you would rather be known as the Naked Truth or a Clothed Lie?

DAY 218

What or who are we in sync with?

To be in sync is to merge with, connect to or become one with. When we've become synced with something or someone; we're joined.Once connected, we're able to move, flow, build, vibrate, etc. together. When there's one, there is the other because they're one. So, what have we connected to voluntarily or involuntarily?

Most connections should bring us power, yet some could drain us. If we've found ourselves synced to any one or thing that's taking our power; disconnect immediately. Better to lose from the disconnect, than to lose oneself.

DAY 219

Zoom zoom, the sound of everything moving around us at warp speed. Our world consists on speed; how fast can we

get it, cook it, develop it, pass it, accomplish it or take it. Zoom zoom. With everything moving fast, people are in a rush to make or take money and the rat race growing daily; we got to slow down before there's a wreck.

Somethings are much better at a slower speed; food sauté, friendships, genuine love, making major decisions and you can think of some more. So, Zoom when needed and slow down when it's lasting.

DAY 220

Somethings just can't be explained. There are somethings we experience that we don't know how to explain it, we just know we saw, felt or know it. Many times we're given names, labels or diagnoses for things that just can't be explained. I remember asking the therapist what's wrong with me. She said, "Why do you think there's something wrong with you?" After months of treatment, I came in one day smiling and told her I got it now. After that final session, she said I wish I could use you as a testimonial of success because you've amazed me. I've never seen or experienced this before in 32 yrs. Then she said, there's no appointment necessary unless you just want to talk because you found you and it's beautiful. (Yes, I'm transparent today; only) I found I'm not destined nor designed to dance to anyone's music but my own. I hear my own drums and that's my sound. Most can't understand me, so they misdiagnose me but that's their problem because I'm free in being me. Never allow anyone or anything to tell you who you are; it's self-contained. Be an original, find you then fall increasingly in love with you. Healing begins with balance; it can't be explained but if you do it, it'll be amazing.

DAY 221

We can be the wind that keeps another person from falling and bring life or hope. It's good to also know that there's someone who we can depend on to catch us.The wind, we can't see it but we know it's there just like the friend who silently holds us up without a word. The wind of a friend is unforgettable, they see what others can't. They feel what hurts inside; they're able to reach out when you feel alone. That wind of a friend will love you from afar but feel closer than those physically there. Can you feel the wind at your back pushing you away from harm, into a brighter day and up above any storm? I found my wind beneath my wings, so that I'm able to soar. Are you the wind that's blowing?

DAY 222

I was prompted to use this as our nugget this morning. Whatever we're facing today; depression, eviction, separation, heartache, sickness, poverty or etc; we're the climate changers. We control our own climate; never give no one or nothing that kind of power over our lives. Step into any and every day owning the climate regardless of what it is outside, we define our inside. If we walk into a room full of negativity, change the climate. Introduce your light, your flow, vibe, energy, swag or frequency but change the climate. If you're not up to that level then leave the room, either way we must protect our atmosphere. Learn to be a climate changer and set the tone for your space. Make it fantastic

DAY 223

My children tickle me when they say that they are so hungry and when I offer them a sandwich; suddenly the hunger isn't that intense. I smile and let them know that they're not hungry enough.

When we want something bad enough and someone offers us an opportunity to get closer to it, if we're hungry, we'll eat. Many don't like crawling in order to walk, so we'll miss the lesson. Let's be willing to start at the bottom, if necessary, to learn all the facets of the position so we can supervise our own. Get hungry enough to plant the seeds, which feed the people that manufacture, own or direct, what we hope to own or connect to in our future.

Be the kind of hungry that sees a vision in the darkest of night and know our daylight is coming.

In all my years, I've never been fired. I've been laid off or not hired but never fired. Until...

I was stressing about a few things not going as planned. Trying to put together the perfect plan to win. How could I juggle a few things around and accomplish success. Wondering if I'll get my dreams fulfilled, touch my finest goals or complete my projects.

Realizing, I had so many fires in ablaze, I needed to prioritize my directions. Who gets paid and who don't? Who gets my attention and who won't? Where's my next flight and why? Ah, I'm working hard here trying to align everything in order until I was told "You're fired".

I'm not in charge and I don't control what's about to happen, I'm just another valuable piece that gets to be in the game.

Well, hello Universe; I'm good now. It's kind of brutal but I now have adjusted.

DAY 224

There's nothing more frustrating than to have put your best in something or someone, only to find it meant nothing.

Sometimes our best isn't valued by those that think so small.

It's been said to never invest in anyone that has nothing to lose. When you are going in with the intentions of bringing your best, expect same; do not compromise or settle.

Know your worth and stand firm on your position.

Whatever is coming to you is designed just for you, no pressure. Have patience and peace while on this journey.

DAY 225

Sometimes we use too much on our energy for negativity. No matter who or what has attempted to interrupt our energy, we do have the power to change or cancel it. Have you walked into an establishment and the got terrible and negative energy or vibes? You're quickly battling this force so that you're able to maintain your positive flow.

Relax, when our power is charged and resonating, we own the position in which we stand. Never compromise who and what you possess to be minimized by anyone or anything.

DAY 226

How many times have we remained silent becuz we felt our question would be viewed as foolish? Only to find that the most foolish thing we've done is to have not asked the question that we desperately need answers to today. Never allow anyone to make you feel that if we ask a question, that it will

be viewed as ridiculous. It may even be the very question someone else is afraid to ask for the same reasons.

If the answer is important to you, then we must ask in order to proceed in whatever our next move is. Regardless of how anyone sees us or thinks about us, we need these answers to make our journey easier or more understandable. So, ask, it will brings us strength.

DAY 227

When you know you're walking on water and able to do things that seems impossible to others, take lessons. We can be able to touch a dream, see the future, stand on mountains and travel limitless places?

When and only then can you become limitless, fearless, endless and fabulous in our destiny. Life is what we make it, how we choose to see and most definitely who we include in it.

Carry the torch and go places others dreamed of being and wish of seeing. It's one thing to be seen, it's another to see but you have arrived when you can do both without skipping a beat.

DAY 228

Every day is a great day to rise up and make it work in our favor. Yesterday is gone, along with its joy or pain but today we can make it better.

We can correct all mistakes, heal from heartaches and administer life within.

Be absolutely great at being your best you and take no negativity in your space.

We're winners prepared for life's battles. There's nothing

coming or in our path that we've not been prepared or trained to overcome. Believe it, receive it and achieve it.

DAY 229

Every problem isn't your problem. Some problems are just problems needing solutions; we're not always the solution.

When we think of problems, we see a matter that looks uncomfortable, can be stressful and will feel unreasonable. But know this, every problem has an answer; some are easy, some available, some doable, others uncomfortable and not agreeable but still the answer.

Instead of focusing on our or any problem, be more directed in the solution.

It's not a problem until we make it one. Adjusting, rethinking, organizing, preparing and maintaining are a valuable key to any problem. Get ready to attack, challenge, laugh, move or reexamine that problem, then go to phase 2. A positive flow brings great powerful energy.

DAY 230

Sometimes we just got to sit back and relax because the world is on stage. Become a quieter student and observe every teacher. Every lesson; good, bad and ugly should teach us something. It's hard to learn when we're not paying attention.

The wrong people can teach us the right things. I've learned to tell those that worked hard to destroy my life and block my future; "thank you". Because I know if they didn't do what that done, I wouldn't have learned a bigger lesson. I rather lose a hundred dollars at this level than thousands at the next one. That hiccup cost me but if I didn't get hindered at

that teacher's class, I would've never arrived at the higher level.

Thank those that hope to see you fail, lose or worse becuz their lesson will promote you. Be a better student and watch how far you'll go from the lesson because EVERYONE IS A TEACHER.

DAY 231

Do you know when you've won, moved on or accepted? It's when the name, the person, place or thing doesn't move us anymore. It's when you ride by, step into, run into or hear whatever or whoever and there are no tears, hate, words or emotions.

Yes, it's like dust; you are aware of its presence but it's meaningless except to remind us to remove it. Dust doesn't get a conversation, water, a ride out or love, it only needs to be gone.

It's like those constant reminders of past pains, bad decisions and blunders; close those doors. Shut out any and everything that seeks to destroy our future, poison our presence and highlight our past failures. Only we can close those doors that we know are keeping us from walking into new ones. Never let a door that needs to be closed to prevent us from getting to the door that seeks to be opened.

If the door is a struggle; slam it and nail it!

DAY 232

What are we saying about ourselves? Words are truly powerful especially when we define ourselves in the equation.

I shall live, I will be prosperous, I'll make great strides in my life, my health will be awesome, and I'll seek truth, positive

people and wholesome things. I'll be careful of what comes out of my mouth, what enters my mind, soul and body and I will guard my spirit from anything toxic. I'm held responsible for my thoughts and will acknowledge my actions; good and bad.

Today, I'll rise above every lie, disease, failure and unhealthy relationship. I'm the master of my life and I won't be persuaded to follow anything or anyone that means me any harm. I'm desirable, valuable, sensational and motivational. I'm above not below blessed not cursed, oil not water and wise not foolish. I'm tearing down walls, building kingdoms and releasing prisoners in my life.

I'm together, complete, perfected and soaring. What about you? Speaking affirmations daily into our lives and day is very important.

DAY 233

We're purposeful, mindful, lovable, enjoyable, spiritual, capable, remarkable and sexual. These are just a few of the qualities we may, should or do possess.

Being filled with so many qualities make our value desirable. So let's be cautious of those who want to enter our circle, become a part of our lives or have personal motives or agendas.

When you're valuable, you're a source(force) to be reckoned with. Our very presence brings and sends, based on the energy that's before us.

DAY 234

The importance of being self-aware. We've accustomed ourselves to believing that it's always another person that should carry the blame or responsibility. This could make us feel better by always shifting the faults on others than to be held accountable for our actions, words and outcomes.

The day we can fully look ourselves in the mirror and say, "That was my fault", "I was wrong", "I got to do better and "I'm sorry", we grow up. The reflection may not be attractive today but as time moves, you'll find that being self-aware is a wealthy commodity.

It'll look on us and it'll build integrity plus character. When we can look back and know that we weren't always the victim but actually played a big hand in the mess we're tangled in today.

I've found myself to be the common denominator to many of my plights that I thought was unfair and wrong. Today, I own it, learn from it and strive to not repeat those beat up roads.

DAY 235

If we're told the sky is blue, we would look up and agree that it's blue. But what if I told you that the sky isn't blue, it only looks blue because of the reflection of the water from the sun, would it change your belief or make you research my findings or words?

Hopefully, you would enjoy my explanation, but it would also trigger your intellect to research my words or beliefs. Everyone has opinions, some stronger than others but no matter how deep or long a lie is; at some point it's revealed.

Cold cases can become solved, mysteries become knowledge, lies become truths and Skippy ain't a butterfly.

Sometimes we got to research the researchers, question the media and refuse to be a deer in headlights.

DAY 236

When we see the beauty of rainbow, we must endure the flow of rain.

Sometimes we desire to see the outcome without dealing with the income. There are so many temporary moments in our lives that we try to make permanent.

We try to stay in the now but realizing now changes the very next second. Enjoy the life we're in, this place we're at while going to the best there is.

Let's not be stunted by temporary pains, hardships, circumstances because we can turn it around. Our present place or position can't define us unless we allow it to. Use whatever is around us and build on it, do not allow it to bury us.

DAY 237

Never compromise who you are to impress people that will never see your worth. It's safe to say that we know thousands of people but know very little about them.

How many people actually know who you are? It's normally only 5 or less that can truly say they've taken the time to invest in our minds, hearts and spiritual being; vice versa. How many really know what your needs are emotionally, intellectually, physically and spiritually? How many are able to see pass the smile and hear a broken heart? Can they move pass the strong personality and know the weakness that's being protected? Will they ever know who we really are or vice

versa?

Meanwhile, we can easily misdiagnose or misunderstand others because we're viewing or being viewed by strangers. Be you, the rest will be revealed in time.

DAY 238

The acceptance of being an individual with imperfections and finding one's self in a world that demands duplications.

I've always been one who dared to be different, make waves, enjoy being unique and finding out what moves me. The problem becomes intense when we're being directed, pushed and sometimes commanded to be the same as those around us so this makes the journey and plight become much more complicated.

We can be rejected because we don't dress, think, act, spend or believe the same. Our greatest gift to this universe is our uniqueness and vibrations to stimulate those around us. Let's not get lost, become discouraged or give up just because someone else is struggling with our identity. Stay true to you.

DAY 239

Can you imagine the conversation between the Eagle and the chicken? It would be the chicken clucking and then dead silence (Eagles won't give time to the chicken(s).

Think about this until it registers; some things shouldn't matter, should be so beneath us that it can't influence our lives. Everything doesn't need to be dignified with a response and the most important one is "there's no relationship" between the two (chicken and the eagle).

We must always remember the relationships that matter

and give no energy to those that don't. The Eagle knows its call, power and purpose so it has no time to spend or energy to waste on chickens. None! Characterized, then prioritize and enjoy the silence in separation.

DAY 240

They say "Opportunity will know but Temptation leans on the doorbell". We seem to be hesitant to one and eager for the other. It seems that the thing we need, we'll linger on it but that which brings gratification for a brief time; carries the better weight.

Today, we got the best doors open for us to achieve, live healthier, be happier, successful and finally be mentally, spiritually, physically and soulfully complete. Yet, what do we do with it? Be careful for those quick fixes, self-ego trips and hidden agendas; they may look or sound better but its end could destroy us. Listen for the light knock.

Peace and Blessings

DAY 241

The day that you find out that your insiders are really your outsiders. Remember that there are some people that walk into our lives to connect to our energy, lifestyles, connections, secrets and power sources.

Once we've been awakened to their plot, deceit and plan; we must quickly close the gate, shut the door and pull the line so that we're not drained, destroyed or damaged any further.

They say" make a fool of me once; shame on you." Make a fool of me twice; clean your mirror".

Live like you've gotten permission to be Awesome.

DAY 242

Sometimes we begin to complain about our splinters and realize that there are those in critical condition. If we're in touch with our surroundings and have the gift of compassion, we'll seek to help those needing us most.

While one wants money to buy a meal, another seeks shelter from harm and still another is battling terminal illnesses.

Because someone is smiling at us doesn't mean they're not suffering within. Homeless people greeting us at the front line with smiles, abused and scared people giving us soft answers and patience and those most stressed are creating an Atmosphere of love.

Yet, we can be so out of touch with thinking of our woes that we miss the opportunity to just be thankful.

DAY 243

Attraction. What are we attracting, what are we attracted to and why? Oftentimes I have had to look at people, places and things with these thoughts in mind.

What are we attracting to our lives? People come into our paths for many reasons; some with hidden agendas, motives, business or pure genuine attraction.

In our observation today, we maybe magnets but let's be careful of who and what we're attracting. Sometimes we must demagnetize or repel from those things or people that mean us no good.

DAY 244

Never apologize for who and what you are; everybody

won't accept you but who has ever been accepted by EVERYONE?

Stop trying to fit in and just live your purpose out. Purpose is what most people ignore because seeking acceptance is greater. Being self-aware, accepting and conscious is our greatest gift to us.

If you're confused about self, we'll confuse others. Understand that once we become fully in tune within, what's going on outside becomes less visible.

Do we really love, embrace and live like we're purposed?

DAY 245

Anything that we do should be done with the full knowledge of its consequences. I rather you slap me with the truth than kiss me with a lie. I believe that honesty is the only policy. I have raised my children to not lie so I had to be truthful. I never told them to lie for me or lie because of me.

I found out that telling and living they truth will keep us honest. Most people tend to lie becuz being truthful could bring painful or unwanted results. Some have of a fear of what the truth could do to a relationship, situation or outcome, so lying seems more feasible. If we live an upright life that full of integrity and honor; truth will be our only option.

Peace and Blessings

DAY 246

As I arrived to have my truck serviced, they asked me if I was familiar with the "waiting area?"

I wish I wasn't but yes, I'm very familiar with the waiting area. It's the place where you must wait and wait and wait. It's

not a likable, attractive, lovable or the place we long for but it's destined. While waiting, occupy the time wisely with profitable, productive and positive energy. It's only a pause not a sentence.

We will all experience the unfavorable and undesirable moments of waiting, so use it and embrace it, it could prevent us from hitting hard knocks down the road.

Blessings and Peace

DAY 247

"One's man junk is another's man treasure" is a phrase we've heard through the years. Today, let's question the observer view; maybe it was NEVER junk; it could've just been hidden from their perception. Many have closed doors on geniuses, leaders, goal makers and powerhouses only because they saw nothing where Something was vivid.

Be thankful, grateful and careful if we're viewed as junk, unworthy or worthless; it may only mean we are preserved for the best that's coming. What one may see could be unsightly because of the eyes that is seeing is impaired.

DAY 248

My children tickle me when they say that they are so hungry and when I offer them a sandwich; suddenly the hunger isn't that intense. I smile and let them know that they're not hungry enough.

When we want something bad enough and someone offers us an opportunity to get closer to it, if we're hungry, we'll eat. Many don't like crawling in order to walk, so we'll miss the lesson. Let's be willing to start at the bottom, if necessary, to learn all the facets of the position so we can supervise our own.

Get hungry enough to plant the seeds, which feed the people that manufacture, own or direct, what we hope to own or connect to in our future.

Be the kind of hungry that sees a vision in the darkest of night and know our daylight is coming.

DAY 249

How many times have someone tried to sell us a dream? When our lives are in desperate need of a right now fix; here comes the dreamer or the schemer. If we're not careful, we'll buy into the lie, hoping that it'll be true; let's not be an easy prey. Never show a heart broken, a mind confused or a life unsuccessful; it's a sure magnet for a predator.

Don't show yourself as weak; be on guard against anything that will try to imprison our future. We must keep our hearts free and clear from any friction that will attempt to entrap us. Monitor the things around, in and by us to make certain that we can be in the right frame of mind and spirit. Blessings.

DAY 250

Most people have trained themselves to say the right things while doing the wrong thing. It takes an exceptional mind to always listen to what they're not saying. It's the hidden things that could cause us pain, loss, misunderstanding and brokenness. Be firm at being truthful even if it's not pleasant or acceptable. When we speak and live honestly; our mouths, hearts and spirits are all aligned and speaking the same things. Listen...

DAY 251

When we think of a home; whether we own, rent, hope for or never had the experience of one, it'll be our foundation today. Our home is so important to us, as it signifies a place that we have security and sense of belonging. Sometimes when our possessions are great, so is our crowd.

This is where we should question our circle; is it a circle of love, opportunists or just temporary vanity?

Our home is our sanctuary and place of comfort, peace and love and to have one is a treasure. Let's make sure the company we keep are the ones we desire to stay.

DAY 252

We must have a plan and a vision. Imagine being blessed with a million dollars and no plan. A year later, we're in need of a great windfall because the lack of respect for money and prosperity. Ever watch the poor go out buy an expensive toy or item and have no food in the home, bills unpaid but looking as if they're the Trumps? It's so sad. It is stated "a fool and their money will soon fall". Can you ride in a paid 1999 car, own your home, have money in bank, debt free and be happy and satisfied? Or are we always trying to keep up with the Jones, the Oprah's, the Gates, the Buffets and etc? Spend little, save much, invest in another's wisdom and bless those that you are led to. Trends change frequently, tattoos make statements you can say, Air Jordan's are made less than $20 yet we pay over $200, who are we trying to impress? Are we in need of that kind of attention from people that wouldn't do anything to help us if we were in need? Let's focus on being grateful for everything we possess, possess what we have and have a plan on the next move.

Wisdom is powerful, knowledge is operational and together it's awesome!

DAY 253

Where are we prioritized in our own lives? Most of us know how to make sure everyone we hold dear is cared yet we neglect ourselves. If we understood that if we fall or break, those that we're holding will lose that foundation. So, we must make sure our foundation is strong, cared for and given the utmost respect. Lift, adorn, encourage, educate, train and empower oneself so that we'll be able to help sustain others.

DAY 254

We'll NEVER be able to fully know why another person does what they do. We're only able to think of what would drive us or interpret from our own level. Another person's makeup or design was created or produce from many outside factors. What a child saw, experienced, felt and endured is what we're observing today. We might not agree with it, can't flow with it or even love it but our opinion doesn't count, it's displayed for us. Let's attempt to be genuine in all that we do and be exactly what we are and make sure those we love can see it. Be extraordinary, an original and full of love and Integrity.

DAY 255

When we have that special thing in our lives that allows us to stand out, it'll cause envy and jealousy. We can be a powerful magnet to anyone desiring to grow and go. If someone

is desiring to grow with us and make their life more prosperous by attaching themselves to us, what a powerful outcome. Are we a magnet or repellent to those that we meet or greet? We can possess the Midas touch or the cursed tree, based upon our knowledge and/or willingness to be trained. Powerful or powerless, is the question that we must ask ourselves when we are confronted with any opposition?

DAY 256

Are you dealing with the spirit of Depression? Most of us have had battles with this terrible spirit that comes to steal, kill and destroy. This demonic spirit will take control over our lives and bring us to an all time low. When we see the spirit of depression has come over our lives, we must fight. We must fight to gain back power and victory over our minds, hearts and spirit.

Shake it off!!! This toxic and deadly enemy will curl up with us at night and rob us of so many tears. Depression will isolate us from every and anyone that could help us find our way back to the light. Once we've identified this monster, deny him access to our minds and fight his words in our mind.

Find your peace, run to your safety and dance your way out of the grips of any negative entity

DAY 257

We are destroyed because of our lack of knowledge. I'm a firm believer that what we don't know can destroy, steal and kill us. Stop believing in all the things we're seeing and begin listening more.

All day if we're focused, we're being taught, directed and

instilled awesome knowledge. Sitting quietly can place us in the center of our universe, imagine that power. Then become that Power; knowledge is one of those powers and if we embrace it, we'll never be the same.

DAY 258

When there's fire burning in us, do we diffuse it or feed it? Some fire needs to be put out before it destroys our life within. Some need to be spread out to end the life that's killing us.

We know the pain of putting out one fire only to have another one ignite. This consumes much of our energy.

Then there's the fire that burns in order to set us in higher power, let it burn. This fire will motivate us, encourage us and empower us to do the greater things that have been invested in us. Where are we?

DAY 259

As our seasons change, are we prepared? Many times in our life takes on a change, has a big upset or is faced with unpleasant issues, we're stressed or uneasy. Many things that come our way has already been filtered out and positioned to get us to the next blessing in life. If we're spending more time our spirit than the distractions of this world; we could be braced for some things. Nothing comes by surprised or without purpose. How can we testify about a miracle we didn't experience?

How do we know that we can come from poverty to wealth, sickness to health, jobless to entrepreneurship, being and nobody to a gift. This comes from those brick walls we hit, those enemies, we thought were friends, from hearing a

doctor's report to being a miracle. NO, nobody enjoys going through the hell but it's the hell experience and torment that gets us smiling in 115-degree weather. Prepare for the season changes.

DAY 260

Many of us can dish it out but few want to spoon it back in. Remember the very words we can quickly send out to others will be needed for ourselves. And I know from experience that spooning it back in is a bit unpleasant.

When encouraging anyone, please keep those words close because when alone, we'll need to remember to encourage ourselves with that same wisdom of words. It's a known fact that the words we send out, will always find its way back to us, possibly not at a good time. But as long as our words were truthful, they'll only heal and bless us.

DAY 261

The blind leading the blind may be the most comfortable place for those who prefer not to know or see the truth. Even though the outcome would be destructive; that place is comforting. Never allow anyone that has no vision, insight or purpose to guide you to success.

Can you imagine taking advice from someone that has no idea, experience or concept of your situation? I can't. It's like asking someone who never have flown, how does it feel in a plane? Or imagine calling a plumber to repair your car. You want someone with some insight to guide you to the right place and lead.

DAY 262

Headlines: Fluoride in toothpaste causes ADD or ADHD in our babies.

Water left in your car can cause cancer because the plastic in the bottles yet we are told to drink warm water because it's better for your health.

Try and guess how many of our vegetables and fruits are hybrid meaning they will put together in some lab test and regenerated for us to eat.

Everything that says organic isn't; it's just a label put on it to get higher prices. They used to be tabloids that would say we were invaded by Martians now we wonder if our neighbors are one.

We work hard to impress people who care less that we're broke or if we have money.

We're being overpopulated by diseases that are terminal and we wonder why. Ever think it could be the food we eating, the air that we're breathing or the people that were trusting?

We are living in a world of Hysteria, panic, fear and confusion and wonder why our children are being bullied every day.

Think about this, if we're not the only world, then why would we think we're the only people? Believe half of what you hear, little of what you see and the rest will align itself up in time.

I'm just saying peace is a place that's always being challenged, wonder why?

DAY 263

Humpty Dumpty sat on the wall and had a big fall. There are so many lessons, questions and thoughts from this one concept of the fall of Humpty Dumpty. Let's fire up some brain cells today.

Why would a fragile egg want to sit on a huge and high wall? How many of us know the climb up is NEVER compared to fall down? What's was so intriguing up on the wall, that couldn't wait for time to show?

Many times we can allow others to bait us into climbing pedestals that has only one way down; that's to fall. Remain humble and grounded or face the fate of Humpty Dumpty.

Fabulous day to you all.

DAY 264

Everyday we're given the chance to make a moment. Whether we choose to make someone laugh, cry, want to be with you or walk away from you; it's our moment.

Everybody wants to laugh becuz laughter is a great medicine; it takes away your problems and gets rid of stress and brings you to another level. Yet sometimes it's time to think about a serious moment and is no time to laugh. So, while we're in a moment, whatever our moment is; choose to laugh or take it serious the outcome is based upon that choice.

Growing up we saw a lot of bad things; we could have chosen to allow those bad things to make us bitter or laugh because we will make it better. Today is our day; laugh or cry is our day and our moment, I'm choosing to laugh.

DAY 265

Some may see me as radical; I know I'm more ridiculous. Becuz I've watched those with so much common sense that they've limited their Faith. Common sense is working with the natural, Faith solely works with the spiritual. Common sense says you only got $50 so be mindful, Faith says that's a seed, plant it and watch it grow.

I'm not radical; I'm ridiculous with my Faith. I'm the woman that planted 90%; almost $9,250 kept the 10%, it was my personal challenge. I had one other person to take the challenge with me and today, we're still living off the increase over ten years ago.

Faith is an action word; it has no fear and knows everything is subject to it. Faith moves and lives impossibly; it's ridiculous. Faith will wink at a Dr.'s prognosis, it'll produce a table in a desert and shield us from our enemies. Yes, it'll build you a home without your money, pay for a car and hand you the keys and open a ridiculous door that has never been open before.

Faith is not lazy, silent, fearful or stressed and loves to be ridiculous.

DAY 266

The world is our oyster as we search for the pearl. Some call it a quest, some a journey yet we should all agree it's a search.

What are we searching for? Whatever it is, our universe possesses it, no matter how big or small. As teens, they are hit with the identity crisis; trying to figure out who and what they're destined to be.

Our identity is so multifaceted; we got so many layers, lev-

els and brilliance that it's hard to center at times.

How many times have we opened an oyster hoping this should contain our pearl? This is deeper than we're able to understand at times but yet we know our answer is near. Every search will bring us closer to sweet truths and priceless information.

Always remember, we're on our own personal journey seeking what will fulfill us, when we find it; hold it dear and don't let go.

DAY 267

Everyone doesn't hear, see or think the same and that's understandable. One baby crawl at nine months, another is walking while another one can read. These different levels have much to do with the surrounding environment. What we're introduced to become our way of thinking, moving and development.

This very knowledge should be the key to what we're choosing to influence our wellbeing and future. Become inquisitive, go beyond the break, seek deep truths, refuse to give up and build success stories. Be the person that will be missed when gone because your presence is rewarding, enriching and loving. If you've left a job, person, place or anything and you're not missed or wished back; that speaks volume about your contribution. Our laughter, smile, honesty, giving, eyes, knowledge and sometimes sweet smell should leave prints, always. When someone says, "I miss you", make sure they mean it.

Be exceptional and a forever memory.

DAY 268

Live a lifestyle that makes everyone wonder what are you doing that they're not? Sometimes in your worst places and your most devastated moments you still look like a hero to someone else. So, keep rising to the top, be like the oil you made to be; it never loses its power to rise.

Some call it the Hustle but you know it to be just a flow. Be great and don't stop.

DAY 269

Acceptance. Most of us are always seeking to be accepted by someone, someplace or somehow. Once we have learned to accept ourselves, the work becomes easier.

We draw our own lines of what's acceptable and unacceptable to and in our lives. When we hear our own music playing inside; we'll dance for the world to see. Too many of us have orchestrated our lives within everyone else's confinement and have no idea who we are.

Freedom always begins inside and once we've accepted ours, it's beautiful. You can't be me and I don't want to be you, we all have our own uniqueness; that's the beginning of acceptance.

DAY 270

How many times have you said something or done something and waited for the connection? Have you ever been on your phone and was talking for a minute before you realized there was no one on the other line? These are the moments when we realize that so many times we are talking to someone

and yet there is no connection. A connection only means that we have been able to identify what each other is saying and receiving it with a strong signal.

When you have connected to like minds you know it, your spirits will immediately rejoice because they're far and in-between. While seeking for those connections many times we will become frustrated and lose hope. Realize today that everything is connected to something you must know what you are connected to. And always remember when the connection is wrong; immediately disconnect.

DAY 271

Find your place of serenity and stay there. There will always be something, someone or some place that will challenge your place of peace, just remain in park. No one can fully understand the journey we've been on, the hits we've taken or the victories we've won. Stop trying to explain to a people who are truly not interested in our wins but just our defeats. We're not here by chance, we're here by assignment. Speak life, success, peace and love into the atmosphere and our universe will bring it to us.

Let's keep on living our best life, against all odds.

DAY 272

Let's understand that we cannot afford to sweat over the small stuff. We have to realize that whatever we find, whoever they are; it is what it is. We are not in control of changing anyone but ourselves. So accept people for who they are and where they are. If they are not what's needed in your positive atmosphere, move forward without them.

We must learn to love Who We Are, what we are and how we are meant to be used in this universe. Smile more, love deep, trust only what you know and build relationships to further your life goals.

The rest is just a journey that we must anticipate that whatever comes is meant for us to learn, build, dismiss and move on. Make everyday special and those who are in your circle will fulfill the gift of your soul.

DAY 273

Everyone has their own way of building their defense. When we hear that our enemy(ies) are planning an attack, we must be vigilant in how we'll win. And it is our goal to win!

Most know the story of the 3 little pigs; each had their own ideas of the win and survival. Yet only one was able to correct errors the others made and defeat the wolf. How many times have we watched others fail at something and we follow that same path? We feel we've got a way around the Tsunami; we can beat the current, we'll land on our feet from 14 stories and then there's someone else who'll tell our story.

Water is water, no matter if it's hot or cold, water will always be wet. Sometimes the results may not be what we're seeking but if we're tuned in and opened, we can avoid mistakes and disasters. Remember the 3 pigs, 3 decisions and 3 outcomes. Has the enemy been tearing down our homes, destroying our dreams and threatening our relationships? Learn how to build stability, ask for help and know that your foundation can stand against all.

DAY 274

When we're bred for greatness, mediocrity won't work. Never measure your lives, accomplishments or visions to anyone else; we're exceptional by ourselves. We all are great at something, find that something and make it our brand, character, outline and stand. Whether a CEO, mechanic, artist, parent or protector; make it reign. Whatever we're designed to do or be, our only failure will be us. Some strive to live long lives but if those years consisted of living meaningless; where's the victory? Don't live a life always in another person's shadow, under someone's thumb or decorating fear; be the greatness you've always needed.

DAY 275

Breathe. Never allow anyone to describe to us what we're looking at. What may look beautiful to one may be disgusting to another. Beauty is in the eyes of its beholder; one person judges from the outdoor, another sees the inside. Have you ever saw weeds that bloomed so splendid? Just breathe; we're not accountable for anyone's vision, desires, mindset or views.

That's peace all by itself.

DAY 276

Babies coming to this world and only know what we are giving them. However way we start them off is what they're going to be expecting. When a baby comes into the world, they mostly come with their eyes closed not able to see clear. It takes time until the child is able to make out what is real. Once their eyes have been adjusted and they can see clear they can

then decipher who you are and what is surrounding them. We are just like those babies we take whatever is given to us and accept it as so until our eyes become adjusted.

Once we're able to see clear and have the ability to know what is real and what is false, we can adjust. Some adjustments take years, some decades but at some point, we all are able to see clearer.

This is called knowing the truth and allowing that truth to set us free. Some would rather not know, and some will seek out.

Some battle with being in darkness and some battle about being in the light. How we mature from these stages remains the question.

DAY 277

What's the forecast? Have you ever noticed that people have their own forecast going on?

We know those who are full of storms and/or disasters. There are those that are windy; however, or whenever the winds blow, you'll find them, never grounded. Then there are those cold and frozen, dark hearts and evil. Some are hot as in sensual or hot as in angry; we should be able to decipher the two. Of course, you're getting the point.

When we see someone coming, a name appears on our phones or knows we're going to encounter them; we already know the forecast, sort of predictable.

Be the kind of forecast that brings sunshine, warmth and a pleasant atmosphere. Read the forecast lately?

DAY 278

Imagine our lives as a puzzle that we're forever putting together. Everyday we're putting things or people in places that they don't belong. We're searching hard for what's missing in hopes we can complete at least the border. Things become difficult when we think we got the right one just to find that it's off by a smidgen. We try forcing things in places that wasn't meant to be filled. We find a piece that resembles an area, but it's not cut out for the position.

We're forever finding a piece to our puzzle, those that belong here, those we move there and those we're still searching for. When we become frustrated with our puzzle's incomplete state; rest a moment, walk away if needed but don't give up the goal.

Strive to be complete and balanced with every piece that we possess

DAY 279

It's been said "Whatever you do the first day of the year; you'll be doing the rest of the year" so… let's do some cleaning.

Yes, let's clean up and out our hearts from some toxic people, relationships and emotions. Let's go into those secret closets and throw out everything that keeps us from being free and blessed.

Let's take the time to do some organizing of what's really important and should have our focus. It's a great day to put our lives in the right perspective so that we follow its route daily.

Nothing from yesterday can override our today unless we allow it. Every mistake we've made, every person we've met

and every moment we've spent is a part of our cleaning up today.

Somethings needs to be thrown away, some reorganized, some need to be prioritized but today is a great day for a new day, wouldn't you say?

DAY 280

Have you ever met someone who could NEVER be satisfied? Whatever they have, it's NEVER enough, and they must have more.

If we pull off the car lot today with a brand-new car, within minutes we'll see one that's really nice. We buy a dream house today while thinking of one we'll build later. It's a pit that can NEVER be filled.

Imagine trying to feed someone hamburger that's craving filet mignon; nearly impossible. Or try having a companion that's ordering champagne with our soda money.

Some cravings are just that, a craving not a need and though we battle with it, it'll pass. We must all know that the most peaceful time in our lives is when we can be satisfied. This doesn't mean you don't still dream or plan, it just means I'm in a place of contentment. I'm able to work with what I possess while applauding those who may have more. I can note that even if what I have isn't much; someone feels envious. There's always going to new; phones, trends, shoes, cars, people, opportunities and possibilities but remember whatever we got was once new to us. Even if it's a used item, when we got it, to us it's new to us.

Find the place of satisfaction and swim there awhile, we may find laughter and peace as well as love. So glad to know what satisfaction feels like, how about you?

DAY 281

They have always told us that " won't we don't know won't hurt us"; that's a lie. There are so many things that we're blind, ignorant or unaware of that can cause us devastation.

Not knowing that there's answers to every problem, if we know where to look or go. If someone knew that the person, they're connected to is someone or something else, would we still be connected? If we invested in a loss venture because of the lack of knowledge, would that be a repeat? Even the law tells us that ignorance isn't a defense. Think about that. What we don't know can and will hurt us, but most prefer not to know.

We all know someone who has told us I rather not know that; I'm dying from an incurable disease, in a relationship with a cheater, where the money came from or any other truths.

Some truths may be temporarily hidden but we have access to it, if we're ready. I rather know a painful truth than be buttered in a lie, without question.

DAY 282

As we stumble with our imperfections, we know it's in the push that we make it. While someone on the outside is trying to diagnose our problems, shortcomings, inadequacies and failures, we know it's in our push that defines our success.

We all have something that we're stumbling with but it's not the near fall that we must focus on, it's the accomplishments that'll speak the loudest.

We may have an ailment, inability, fear, physical plight or whatever but the push is bigger. We've got pause at times, cry at times, and fight or become humble but we give up the push.

Our will to push will ALWAYS speak volumes, ALWAYS. Stumble on but don't stop the push.

DAY 283

Let's not be concern with the doors that are closed and positions that are filled. We got so much to give, doors to open, stories to tell and positions to fill. We're fabulous in our own ways, greater beyond compare and capable to being outstanding. So, let's fill the position, there's several openings. There's a position open for us, NEVER believe that we're not qualified, acceptable or destined to fill it.

DAY 284

We'll NEVER be everything for everybody, but we'll ALWAYS be something for somebody.

We're surrounded by so many opportunities, advancements, hindrances, hurt, pain, love, joy and list forever continues. Yet, decide on what we want to birth out, be filled with, entangled in or destroyed by. Our universe is a fertile ground, atmosphere and welcoming power that we can either embrace or reject.

So, let's use our words wisely because every word we speak is planted; good or bad. Our atmosphere is listening,

DAY 285

We've all been given some kind of talent or gifts but what we choose to do with it, is our decision. We can make excuses of why we're unable to succeed or use our inner talents and/or gifts and become phenomenal.

I've seen those without limbs overcome obstacles, those without one of their senses yet it wasn't the excuse of failure, it was the reason to succeed.

We can always find the reasons why it won't work instead of seeking why it will. Take your talent and multiply it, be the success story that will feed, encourage, embrace, unite, empower and bring wealth to those connected to us.

It's our story; we make the deciding factor on how long, strong or wrong it'll go. So...

DAY 286

I've always loved being a secret giver and enjoying the public blessings. If we're working to be helpers or angels for others, we don't need an audience, cell phones or media. All we need is the right heart and spirit so we can do our best to replace frowns with smiles. Try giving anonymously, loving unconditionally and touching lives frequently. There's no greater satisfaction at times than sharing our best with those with so little. We are the world!

DAY 287

We know the truth can be digested, understood and told many ways.

The root is the truth, but the ground broke something new and the world only sees the results. Yet, the truth still remains deep in the roots that most don't care about or take time to explore.

Once the truth is open, seen or told, there's a beauty to those that enjoy the unadulterated truth. There's something about the truth, no matter how many times we tell it, it will never change or become mixed up, it'll hold up forever.

Keep telling it, despite anyone that finds it distasteful.

DAY 288

Our circle will always change when we change. Things that we were comfortable with before, makes us walk from now. The jokes that use to be funny, now becomes disturbing. The people that we felt were amazing and true, now flicker in the background. It's called life and if things aren't being rearranged from time to time, then that could be our problem.

DAY 289

Let's stop expecting people to give us something that they don't possess. We not only frustrate ourselves, but we frustrate the other person. A person can only give what they possess. If they only got $30, asking for $700 is not only a hardship but clearly almost impossible. Looking for love, security, peace, knowledge or any other desire maybe exhausting when the one we seek it from is either clueless or fruitless. So, what are you going to do?

DAY 290

We could always make assumptions but the moment we make judgement based on that, we're erred. Our outlook on someone or something is personal not factual.

Every tree is KNOWN by the fruit it bears; trees can't lie. Orange trees must bear oranges; pecan trees must bring pecans and so on. We don't have to assume, all we have to do patiently wait and the fruits will speak for themselves; good,

bad and etc.

Sitting in the front seat in class doesn't make us smarter nor does sitting in front pew make us holier. Our position can be adorned but our lifestyles will bear witness to our connections. Be a living tree that brings life

DAY 291

Sometimes the very thing we're running from is what we need to build us. Things that make us uncomfortable could be the bridge that will bring us over. Being uncomfortable is a temporary state not a permanent position. Let's ask ourselves why are we uncomfortable with this thing, person or place then learn how to overcome that state.

We're being prepared to graduate but before we can accomplish that goal, we must be willing to endure many challenges. These battles aren't to show us how incompetent we are but to let us see our current weaknesses so that we can be stronger.

Every wind can't blow us down, every fire can't consume us, every fight can't knock us out; we must use our most difficult times as our stepping stones to empowerment. We're built for this

DAY 292

No matter how little or how much we possess, if we aren't wise, it won't last. Everything must change at some juncture in life; nothing is intended TO remain the same. When our changes come, we're expecting great outcomes not that things will worsen.

Let's remind ourselves that our possessions are to be used,

distributed, cared for or gained for purpose. Let's be wise in whatever we've been blessed with, always.

DAY 293

Let's talk about the walls in our lives. We repeatedly hit walls throughout our lives, sometimes in frustration, others in confusion and then those that we're grateful for.

We've built our own personal walls that put limits on us and others. These walls can be permanent or temporary, but they're placed to limit, confine, post warnings or set boundaries. Today, we want to be clear about our walls and reasons.

I'm being totally thankful for the walls, rails and boundaries in my life that wouldn't allow me to go but so far. Even when we wanted to try things, go places or become someone else, we had walls. These walls protected us from what we didn't know that was on the other side.

Rails on the roads are there for protection, fences are to set perimeters and walls are to separate as it also stops. Whatever the wall that's around us; self-made, God designed, or others constructed, there's a reason and a purpose, proceed with caution or respect the structure.

DAY 294

Just as we frown down on someone else's lifestyle, problems, dysfunctions and mental state; someone feels the same about us.

Wherever we are in our daily walk, we'll meet us so patience is a virtue. That person that's forever annoying us, those that aggravate the most out of us are truly building character in us.

Some could call us cold, direct, bipolar, selfish, critical, forgiving, trusting, and lovable or whatever but labels can be corrected. Many times, while waiting in the grocery line, Dr's office, lunchroom, listening to staff, friends or family, we'll find moments to mellow down instead of escalating from 0-100.

Let's find time to inhale, process and re-examine the situation before laying down our hammer of judgement.

DAY 295

Ah, remember the times someone would say "you'll never miss your well until your water runs dry"? That is a true statement that we often need to remind ourselves of.

The thought that today could be the last day we have our sight, hearing, ability to walk or breathe on our own. Some also know that we're only one paycheck from being broke or homeless.

What if our home caught up in flames today, our only car breaks down, and we're given a bad Dr's report? Where would be without the person that always got our back, bails us out and steps in without complaints?

The things we take for granted need to be truly appreciated today because we just don't have any idea what or who could be excluded from it?

Take a few minutes to be truly thankful for everything, yes even the bad cause we're able to change anything. Nothing is impossible, if we can believe it; nothing.

DAY 296

Whether we're Ruth, Esther or Nefertiti; we were created to adjust to change and be groomed for excellence. It's not how we started out, it's how we've finished and refused to quit.

Many are born in poverty but saw, created and opened doors to prosperity. Some were fortunate enough to have been brought into this world wealthy yet lost it all with just one wrong move.

We've seen the rich with no class and the poor full of etiquette; amazing. All it takes is the desire to go from a zero to a hero. To no longer roam the streets but now employing those off of those same streets. To coming from a life in Detention centers, foster care and addictions to now building second chance enterprises for success story.

We may have beaten into the ground, stripped of our identity or sculpted into a negative but with the right guidance; we can master our life with everything positive.

Keep going, don't believe the lies, we're another powerful story waiting to be written.

DAY 297

Some are admired for staying, others are congratulated for leaving. We all make decisions based upon our ability to process, proceed and live with outcome.

Never allow anyone to rush us into anything we're not ready for because it will be us dealing with it not them. Whether it's a job, relationship, business venture or etc, we must make choices that will bring, keep or allow us to be at peace. Maintaining our peace should be priority and without question and non- negotiable.

Whatever stands before us today, seeking advice is good

but the final decision is ours to live with so be wise.

DAY 298

There's nothing more frustrating than putting together a project and find we done something wrong. There's bolts left-over, the last piece doesn't fit, they final project doesn't look like the picture. What happened? We didn't follow the instructions.

Every day, we're met with guidelines, instructions and task that we should meet in order to receive our goal, purpose and promise.

If we're given sound instructions to help us become better, healthier and wiser; apply it. Much of our downfalls come from not following the directions that we've been given or not following it fully.

Whenever we're questioning our outcome, let's check our income.

DAY 299

Most people judge us from where we are, not knowing where we could've been. We've listened to much talk about the regrets of not accepting opportunities that were presented to us. Yet as we travel through life, we realize some roads, doors, people and presentations should've been postponed. In our popcorn world, we feel what we want or desire is for is NOW but in all essence we've had to wait for purpose. It is ours but not now.

Sometimes we must wait to mature, be grateful, be humble, be positioned or just be ready but all this comes in our waiting. Let's be thankful for the bridges over troubled waters, the milk that spilled and the life lessons we've been taught. They all come to make us better not bitter.

Be kind, understanding and determined to live life with loveable intents. Those that don't know us shouldn't impact us.

DAY 300

Privileges. Sometimes people get upset because they're unable to get the same perks and advantages as another. When we join the military, we're given certain privileges that civilians don't get. Working in a Union gives us privileges, being born in a family gets those special treatments and the list is endless.

We all have some form of privileges that another person doesn't get. Rank has its privileges and so does membership. What are we signed into or connected with that grants us access to the GREATER?

DAY 301

The power of the three L's in life; Live, Laugh and Love. Live with no regrets, Laugh instead of crying and Love in spite of.

The life we live is ours to sail, if it becomes a shipwreck, we must own that too. Let's choose to laugh instead of crying so that we heal our pain, tear down our enemies and overcome mountains.

Love the things that matter, the people who we hold dear and every day that we've been given an opportunity to be in it.

DAY 302

Every day is a great day to be thankful even during trying times.

Today, we might want to remind ourselves that we have so much to be thankful for. In a world that wants to magnify perfection, we know we're living proof of imperfection. Because of this, we're shamed by our dysfunctions and inability to conquer all areas of our lives.

MIA (Mental Illness Awareness) is looked down upon when in all actuality it lies within our perimeter. Years ago, it was ignored, laughed at, buried, locked away or considered taboo. Schools, family, friends, children and life issues have misdiagnosed, failed, misunderstood or abandoned us.

Love and patience are highly recommended in order to embrace those struggling with this unspoken illness as it's also needed for us too. Whether we acknowledge, accept or ignore it, dysfunction has the ability to function each day despite the battle.

We may not wear a sign, tell the story or seek the help but it lives. Hats off to Taraji P. Henson who has opened the door to erase the shame of Mental Illness by opening up while succeeding in the world. We all have our demons, ignoring them doesn't help, confronting them brings balance.

DAY 303

Whatever we're facing, having to deal with or paid dearly for; it was to groom us.

Grooming will cut here, shave close there, remove and then clean for the finishing touches. How many times do we find ourselves being groomed into being a better person?

Life's dilemmas push, pry, beat, shake and move us in so

many ways just to get us where we need to be. Be thankful for the journey and the Master grooming.

DAY 304

While people are admiring our strength, we're correcting our mistakes. We rise up every day checking our weaknesses for any tears, wounds and open doors that need to be repaired. Then we can be ready for our daily task which begins with inspecting our armor.

Our armor must be in pristine condition because it's our guard from every weapon, battle, folly, mistake and person seeking to enter our lives.

Being strong is what we have learned to do and be while needing comfort also. So remember iron needs to sharpen iron and don't make light of the strength that's been given because many seek it.

DAY 305

Would you rather be known for who or what you are? Sometimes, people may forget our names, but they can always remember our position, character, lifestyle and love. It brings a smile to face when I can think of the nameless people who gave, inspired or changed my life. I never got their name, but I'll always remember what they did and affected my life.

Be the kind of person others will ALWAYS smile about, talk about and plant seeds becuz of what you've done in or to their lives. It's not so important to me that you know who I am (byname) than it is that you've been blessed by what I am.

DAY 306

Whatever dark clouds may be hanging over, storms that's raging and fire that's burning; please know It's going to be Alright. Life brings us temporary events that we must not make permanent stands on.

A fire will die out, the storm will eventually cease, and healing is a process. This doesn't mean that there won't be damages, scars and memories but believe that It's Going to be Alright". Everything is absolutely going to be okay (my son's song; LP).

Sometimes through bitter tears, hurtful words and intense pain; look in the mirror and repeat It's Going to be Alright until we can believe it.

DAY 307

Let's be aware that because someone has nothing to say, doesn't mean that they don't know anything. A quiet person shouldn't be viewed as being ignorant; most are very wise. Their wisdom reminds them when and what to speak and to whom to speak to.

Silence can be golden, stress free and even attractive to those needing a listening ear. Sometimes if we sit quietly, we can hear so much to apply, learn, discard or possibly participate in.

Every conversation does not need our input.

DAY 308

Leave your home like you're coming back but if you don't make it back, leave it like you cared.

Absolutely!

Whatever or whoever you love; departing sometimes is difficult, sad or hesitant. When we choose to walk away, let go, call it quits or dissolve that comma or period, do it with wisdom. Some doors are permanent and others temporary, so how to approach or close every door.

Leave without drama, hatred and malice because we never know if that door is ever needed again. Also, when going through a door, grace it, bless it and learn while present because nothing is forever.

We were taught to make our beds, tidy up our home and discard anything you don't want found by anyone.

Make each day pleasant in the meeting and the farewell.

DAY 309

I kept flirting with Success until today I got a date; tomorrow I'll have the name.We all know the desire of having something or someone so bad that we'll move whatever mountain to get it, right? It's like the connection is unexplainable, the fire is uncontrollably, the time is unimaginable, but the reach is attainable.

We know the feeling of failure, loss and setbacks yet these things can't stop us from believing in the impossible.

Remember no one else was chosen to be you, do the things you do, make the steps you've done so succeed. Be the success story that will leave the legacy of hope to remind anyone that purpose has a plan, and our name is on it.

DAY 310

Before we allow anyone to tell us what we lack, remember only you truly know you.

We may not possess what another individual is seeking for, that's ok, and we can't be everything for everybody. Making others happy could leave us sad. Be wonderful, stunning, unstoppable, full of integrity, lovable and without question; NEVER BE ANYONE'S OPTION.

Have an absolutely amazing day.

Enjoy the journey!

DAY 311

There are some things that I simply can't do or unable to do well but the things that I can do, I'm just "Awesome."

This is my personal quote that motivates me to not be concern, jealous or competitive with anyone. It's not our attention to our dysfunctions that can empower us but our ability to excel because of them.

DAY 312

When we get to the place of frustration, hurt, burnouts, confusion and being totally overwhelmed; hit reset.

Reset is the inner button used to erase everything and start over. Our brain can become so overloaded that if we don't rest properly, it'll shut itself down. Resting allows our brain time to rejuvenate itself to a fresh, start. How many times have we desired a fresh start, a new beginning and a chance to make change? Within our grasp is the reset button, let's use it.

Job didn't work out, reset. Spent money foolishly, reset. Body fighting us, reset. Relationship was a disaster, reset. Wrong decision, wrong move, wrong partner and wrong life choices; simply hit reset. We make things complicated that were meant to be easy, just reset. Blessings to you

DAY 313

To lie or tell the truth? To go or stay? To love or hate? To do or don't? To cry or laugh? To be or not to be?

Those are the questions, to be the relationship or out? To be there or here? To stand or sit? To spazz out or remain calm?

Every action gets a reaction but how we respond is the answer. Sometimes we must be unpredictable to those hoping to push our buttons. Let them know that the button has been disabled.

Be in control of what you choose to be.

DAY 314

Once I was told, "you're looking great, how you do it?". I replied I lost 230lbs, they said "girl, when you gain that much weight, I never saw you that big?" I said, "I got rid of him, he weighed 230lbs ". To some that's humorous but for others it's real.

Sometimes our biggest weight is what we're carrying. We're carrying people, their problems and a mass of other things that we just need to let go of, release into the atmosphere or lose.

Drop some headaches, stress, leeches, bad habits and bad investments then watch our life grow. Many of us are trying to carry some people or things into our future that are only dead

or extra weight.

Want to lose weight fast; stop feeding, excusing and holding on to what's unnecessary weight. Just saying

DAY 315

Every day is an absolutely great day to position ourselves in a place to make history speak volume. So let's live a life that someone can read or hear about and say "wow, they're awesome, I want to be that one day". Be unstoppable, unbelievable, incredible, remarkable, impossible, desirable, sensational, profitable, untouchable and lovable. They may not understand our flow, touch our flow, stop our go or have pictures to show but they know. Fear pushes us, Favor embraces us, enemies chase us, haters try to duplicate us and still we reach plateaus that were restricted to us. Let's be the visionary that made it because we NEVER stopped believing, pushing and standing.

DAY 316

We're forever connecting and disconnecting throughout our lives. Whether it's for wisdom, curiosity, troubles, popularity, pressure, acceptance, love, obedience, maturity or ignorance, we're placed in this position.

When directed by our spiritual being, we're far more able to make the right decision than by our hearts and minds. Making critical moves with temporary tools usually will cause us to make foolish steps that could cost us dearly.

But spiritual guidance will lead to the right doors to connect or disconnect. Sometimes connections today must be disconnected tomorrow or vice versa. We must always be spir-

itual connected in order to know who, what, when or where to connect or disconnect.

DAY 317

The power of the words "Thank You". When we pour out our best unto others and we give from our hearts; repayment of the golden words Thank You are appreciated.

Many will take and even feel entitled to whatever we possess yet few feel the need to express gratitude. Thank you is such a heartfelt response that we should use frequently. Let's try to make it a part of our daily conversation.

DAY 318

So, which you we rather be, the lender or the borrower? Most would say, the lender yet hate to lend. What's the purpose of possessing things if we're not willing to lend it out?

Yes, we've got more than enough yet do we enjoy giving as we do receiving? If we love being blessed, we must also love blessing others.

An awakening comes when we become tired of giving, loaning and blessing others, we can then exchange places and become the borrowers. No one likes being in the position of having nothing or very little while living at the lowest level so when we ask for prosperity, expect to lend.

Why ask to be a lender and refuse to do so? This could possibly lead us back into or never coming out of poverty.

If we the outpouring, let's be cheerful in our position of giving. Think about this deeply.

DAY 319

As I operated in the supervisory authority, one of my most frequent phrases was "Just make it happen".

Many times we find do many excuses as to why something didn't go through, things weren't completed or why we gave up. When we've got a project, vision or plan, we must work on seeing it manifested even if we're unable to do it ourselves. Whether we're organizing an event, running a marathon, having a spectacular day set or etc, we need to organize the right people in the right position to Make it Happen. When we place an order online, we're not expecting anything but our product to arrive, we've got no idea the circumstances at the plant; we're interested in only our results.

Remember this when we put our word to something, can we Make it Happen? People aren't concern about our headaches, pains, loss, personal dilemmas or setbacks. They're only concern about, can we Make it Happen? When we pray about a situation, our only thought or need is Make it Happen. It may take a long period, we could possibly lose some people along the way, we might have to carry some stripes but in the end; Just Make it Happen is our request.

How many of us today are waiting or needing the Make it Happen results?

DAY 320

We must be able to see it before we can be it. We have got to see ourselves going into it, fulfilling it and changing it before we can accomplish it.

Provision will be made when we can envision ourselves there. No matter how big, how far, the cost or object, it's all possible when we move towards it. Whatever is needed to

complete our vision will be provided when our Faith is utilized. Believe it and the achievement will follow, sometimes slowly, sometimes with timely lessons but still they'll manifest.

DAY 321

Whatever we decide to do, be or go, don't allow anyone to box us in. We're created and formed to be unique, yet we're told being different isn't acceptable, by who's code?

Dare to be different is the only code I choose to live by. Whatever has been poured inside of us is meant for us to take this power and utilize it. The biggest misconception in our world is we must mimic someone else's lifestyle, behavior, trend or marketing. Wear, walk, talk, sing and most importantly live as we've been designed or called.

Ignore the hypocritical stares, the unimportant whispers and the secret haters. What truly matters is how comfortable are we in the skin we're in? Let the world know that there's no box that can contain us, DON'T GET BOXED IN; refuse it.

Be free to be you and be the best you that this world could ever meet. Love everything, we can be and own it with pride. If approached by the way we are, remembering anyone can blend, being exceptional takes finesse, skills and boldness so everyone won't do it. Don't box me in

DAY 322

When we become tired of being stuck in the same place, situation or with the same people; we'll shift. We've got more influence over our own lives than anyone. When it doesn't fit, shift. When the words become repetitive and the future looks dim; shift. When the door closes, passion dies or life changes…. shift.

We don't have to stay here, there's always room to shift. Never allow anyone, anyplace or anything to keep us stuck in a place that's bring us discomfort, pain, stress and negativity.

Let's position ourselves to shift our lives into BETTER

DAY 323

Most of us know the hesitation of facing obstacles; will it overtake us or will we overpower it? Everything that we are working to accomplish in life comes with obstacles. Obstacles are temporary structures set to try our patience, mindset and determination in fulfilling our goals. Never allow any obstacle to make final decisions for our purpose, plan and promise.

Learn to move forward with the passion given and expect oppositions and obstacles, they will only build character. Be encouraged and know that we're built to conquer all obstacles. Blessings to you.

DAY 324

Let's make sure the life we live be the one we want to be remembered for. The song that says "may the life I live speak for me" be our everyday decision.

Live a life that brings you fulfillment and peace, the rest

will come together.

Don't be consumed with competing or living up to anyone else's plateau, create your own

DAY 325

Being brave is having the ability to say No when others are saying yes. To walk away from anything or anyone that we're attached to and desire but know it's draining us.

To rise up early each day and fight battles that bring fear but we know we must combat. Be brave enough that every enemy knows that we're not going to bow, give up, compromise or submit. We may tremble but we'll engage, we might cry but we hold our position, we could hesitate but we'll NEVER lose our ground.

There's no bravery without fear and there's no win without some form of confrontation. Be brave

DAY 326

Let's Never allow anyone else to convince us of who we are. People have a way of labeling us in many areas of our lives; socially, economically, spiritually, physically and mentally. Don't let the labels make us. It's not what others think, feel or believe about us, it's what we know of ourselves.

As a man (woman) thinks so is he. No matter what anyone else is saying, what are we saying about ourselves?

Speak life, healing, peace, prosperity, wisdom, freedom and purpose over in our own lives. We possess everything we need to succeed regardless of any of our shortcomings. We're powerful within our own mind to accomplish all of our goals.

Forget the labels and become unstoppable in the achievements we've got before us.

DAY 327

We should live a life before and with others that is fulfilling and one that speaks volume. Live so that when you're gone or have moved on, you'll be missed.Live a life that will make it difficult for anyone else to duplicate or erase. Be awesome and own the right to being unique. Live the prosperous life, full of greatness, peace, genuine love and pure joy despite any and all obstacles. Let's fill our life with people that will support, protect, cherish and value us.

Have an absolutely amazing day

DAY 328

Every victory isn't easy. Many watch a team play and at the end they would say, they lucked out, but they won.

It doesn't matter what the challenge, risk, near miss or outcome; a win is a win. We must remember, we may be dismembered, discombobulated, displaced, discharged or discouraged during the battle but when it's a win, it's a victory.

Our victories may bring us out with deep scars, hurtful memories, broken relationships and near-death experiences but staggering we still got a victory. Fight to the finish, believe until the end and go the last mile because Victory is in our DNA.

DAY 329

Why don't we always feel our Higher Power and its presence? If the presence is really an open door, why does the door sometimes feel like it's been shut on us? There are a lot of reasons why we could feel far away, but none of those reasons is because the Power has pulled away from us.

Our love for us is unchanging, unending, and unconditional. No matter what we do, we must always love us. Our love is the greatest love! Even still, we can't expect the Power to come into our lives uninvited. It's not going to overwhelm us with the presence if we haven't asked for it. We have to invite in and truly become a part of lives, in our hearts and faithful.

We want participation, not idleness. Life isn't going to knock on the door and drag us through it. its presence is an open door, but it's up to us to step through it. If it's what's we want and has provided the door for us, it's on us if we walk in. No one is to blame for us not walking into our destiny and calling. Seize the opportunity whilst you still have the chance to!

DAY 330

JAM; Just A little More. When our bodies are fighting against us; J.A.M. Heart broken, mind tired, finances depleted and the world banging at our door; J.A.M.

We must cheer on each other by speaking encouragement Just A little More.

Let's remind ourselves that we've got just a few more steps, days, opportunities and possibilities before we're out of the rut. Hold on Just A little More and things will change either outside or inside but there will be a change. J.A.M.

DAY 331

Knowing when our seasons have changed. Just as we must prepare for a season change, we also must be in sync with the change.

Every season requires change and if we're paying attention, we'll survive each season while being thankful for lessons imposed. Spring is our moment of new life that the summer will harvest in. Fall tells us to let go of what's behind and use whatever we've gained as a valuable asset.

Winter will put to sleep or lay to rest anything that needs to be quietening down. Respect and work within our season in hopes of tearing down, building up, gathering and removing what's purposed for our lives. Everyday can be our New Season

DAY 332

We must know what doors are opened and which are closed before proceeding. How many times have we opened doors that should've remained closed and how many open doors, we refused to go through?

Wisdom comes when we know there are doors all around us waiting to be opened or closed yet making the right decision before moving forward.

Remember there have been many doors that's been opened for us and closed to others as well as many closed doors to us but opened to others.

Understand each door and its purpose.

DAY 333

Most of us know we've got some things in our lives that we're working diligently on. We've got some personal mess ups, bad decisions and situations that we're trying to master. With this being said, as we're growing out of bad choices, we must know when to disengage from adding on more weight.

There's always someone ready to add on to our current situations and we got to know when to pump our brakes. If we aren't careful, we'll be medicating because of someone else's weight, ignorance, bad choice or etc.

Know when to say NO and hold on to it. No matter how many times we've said yes, the first time we say No, we're condemned. Live daily the stress-free life

DAY 334

How many of us would spend money, time or energy to go hear someone that doesn't move us or bring anything positive into our lives? Yet, we'll give platforms, podiums and blow horns to those that want to bring us down, tear at our flesh and destroy our lives. Today, reconcile within and decree No More will anyone or thing be spoken from our lips that defines negative impact in our lives. Whoever or whatever has tormented, attacked, attached or attempted any malice at us, are dismissed.

Whenever we're complaining or talking about the things that are going wrong, that are what we surrender our moment to. Ignore all things that don't encourage, support, bring us peace, and make us smile or stands to be magnified. Whatever we give time to anyone or anything by conversation or concentration; it owns us for those moments. So let's make sure all time is positive and of a great report. Start the process one

day at a time and begin it today.

We'll no longer acknowledge anyone, any place or anything that seeks to take our peace, focus, purpose or flow. Take back our lives by muting theirs.

DAY 335

While some are practicing how to mean (grille) in the mirror, we must continue to smile. Some people get a kick out of knowing they've turned our world upside down but let's refuse to let anyone steal our smile.

When they're trying to jab us, lie to or on us, walk away from us or attempt to set us up; smile. Don't just smile but bring on the killer smile; it's that smile that can destroy every plot or plan. After a hard battle, long crying night or broken relationship, find the smile that'll triumph and bring hope to others who need this encouragement. Smiling is an exercise that works and will always confuse any enemy, breakup, Dr's report, eviction, financial woes and life's bitter hits. Your smile is needed.

DAY 336

At some point in our lives, we must be close enough to a mirror to know it's time for change. The worse thing a person can do is not know when, how and what to change when it's time.

When we're able to reevaluate our lives, we should always see room for improvement, discarding and management. Change should always be embraced. When we realize that there are things in our lives that need to be adjusted, removed, added or upgraded, we then must change them. We begin

with our health, serenity, finances, inner circle, directions and spiritual connections.

Eachshouldrefineusinsomeplaceinourlifetoabetterchange. Ask yourself today, is today a great day to begin changes that will make your life better, freer and more prosperous?

DAY 337

Somewhere and sometimes in life, we're given a bitter cup to drink from. When our table is set, we're looking for the most delectable food to eat. In our lives we're faced with some very difficult obstacles that we wish we could pass.

We fight illnesses, losses, curses, friends, family and foes to a point of giving up but instead we become stronger, wiser and better. Our bitter cup isn't attractive, welcoming or easy to swallow but it's still ours to take. Whether we've been presented with this cup, drank from this cup or comforting someone else who had experienced the pain from this bitter cup, this cup is coming.

In this bitter cup is hope during difficult times, comfort in crying times, peace in tormenting times and healing during challenging times. This cup is bitter and unpleasant to the taste but in all aspects, it's necessary for a bigger moment.

Drinking from this cup will bring us humility, love, direction, prosperity and training for greater things to come. Don't get lost on the bitter cup, become aware of the many great things that are poured in us by it.

DAY 338

When speaking to someone of importance, always look into their eyes; listen to the soul not the words. Many people can talk and say things that their heart is far from. It becomes easy to talk on the phone, social media or text but when talking face to face, most want to avoid eye contact.

The soul can't lie not matter how hard we may try to hide its truth. Look through the windows of the soul and we'll find what's hidden; good or bad.

DAY 339

We all know about that thorn that's in our flesh because it reminds us daily with its pain. Time and time again, we're seeking answers in removing our painful thorn. A thorn will bring us pain, shame, hurt, stress, fear or any other annoyance. This thorn will interrupt our sleep, relationship, confidence, Faith, love, focus, health and desire to move forward. This thorn will shake a city, destroy a marriage, isolate our dreams and brings us into captivity if we allow it to dictate or dominate our lives.

A thorn is a constant reminder of an area in our life that's been attacked. It jabs at us, brings unwanted attention to us and seeks to overtake us but we still have the final say.

We can privately battle our thorn or publicly expose it but either way, we must not bend or bow to its purpose. We got a thorn and it's true that it won't let up, yet we know we're graced. What has been sent to challenge us is also the message to prefect us.

We've been graced with this thorn because someone else's thorn may be fatal for us. We don't like nor enjoy this thorn, but we've got to master its plan to weaken by becoming strong.

Whether you're overworked, overweight, overwhelmed or overcome, don't be overtaken

DAY 340

BELIEVE. One simple word with so much meaning! Every day we believe. We believe that we're going to get paid, we believe we're going to wake up in the morning; we believe what doctors tell us, we believe that when we go to turn the light on that they'll come on. We believe in so many things and people, but our belief can be so easily wavered or even destroyed. We have to remember that through anything and everything, we must be good, and things will always come through for us.

DAY 341

Protection. How many of us are qualified protectors? Anything or anyone we love; we automatically protect.

Watching our babies begin to walk, we stand close enough to catch them before or when they fall. Our homes protect us from the various elements, and we're protected from unforeseen obstacles, heart aches, tragedies, diseases and other wicked enemies.

We need to remind ourselves that we're NEVER alone and unprotected. We must stop looking at the things that is or has happened and understand we've been protected by things that hasn't.

Imagine about to trip and a hand catches us, could've been in a place but got delayed by protection. Always know even when we can't see it, believe it or feel it, we got protection.

Inhale don't get perplexed and know our protection is ALWAYS on duty; that's love.

DAY 342

Many people may be confused about who they are and what their purpose in life is, so they're easily led down dark paths; if they're not enlightened. When we're not sure about our destination, purpose and identification, we can get lost quickly.

Know whoever it is we've placed in the front to lead or guide us, make positively sure they can get us where we're trying to go. When anyone is granted the opportunity to direct us, they must be trustworthy.

Trust is a powerful word and duty that not everyone can hold. So, there are times we must look in the mirror and repeat to ourselves "Trust Me, I'm the Boss ". No matter what's presented, we make the final decision for our life. We must trust our self and remain Boss over our lives as we're lead spiritually.

DAY 343

Be careful what you ask for, you just might get it.

Seeing many people write posts online about many things, I've witnessed their plea answered. Sometimes it's answered in a way that they weren't quite prepared for. So, when we began to operate the ASK principles (Ask, seek, Knock), expect an answer at the door. Write it, claim it and receive it. Be as wise as a serpent and as innocent as a dove.

DAY 344

Imagine trying to do wrong and get a change of heart to do right. How many times have we plotted or declared to do wrong and end up doing right? The argument we were set to start, the date we were going to cancel or the person we vowed to never communicate with again somehow gets changed.

We should be glad that interventions happen in our lives that give us another opportunity to get ourselves together.

Think about all the people we would've banished from the world, disconnected from our presence and took for granted. There's something about our character that makes do right, be honest and love beyond barriers. This speaks about our character, which is priceless and rare.

Let's let our character define us even when our friends won't.

DAY 345

Why are we called warriors yet believe we shouldn't engage in a war? Why do we think we must be weak and always be submissive and defeated? At what point do we conclude that this means war and take back EVERYTHING that's been stolen? Some confuse meek with weak, humble with crumble and fight with flight.

We're in a daily war, we're more than conquerors and yet many of us submit instead of fighting. There are spiritual and natural battles; do we use natural and spiritual weapons?

A thought for today not a debate

DAY 346

Everyone knows the feeling of freedom when it's given, introduced or experienced.

Imagine being burdened, refused or restricted for a long period of time and finally the gates or doors open. That's a feeling no one can take from us nor know the full magnitude of its power. Freedom.

Paying off that debt, being released from Dr.'s care, finally gave birth to the vision and etc, that's a freedom only you can know.

But what if we lived everyday as if those same gates have or is opened? Ok, the gate is open. Live

DAY 347

As we prepare for a possible category 4 storm, we think about the strong winds. With these strong winds, we can expect many things to happen and change. Lives will be affected, and the world is watching, praying and bracing.

We look at strong winds and some panic others trust. Some think about the winds of life that remove our enemies out of our paths. The winds will bring down trees in order to build up cities. These storms can cause even evil and wicked people to bow down and know they're not God. History says storms will shake up a world and our world may need to be reminded of what power they really have when a much stronger power is coming.

Plans are changed, people are awakened and know that there's a God in control. Be safe and blessed while trusting the Master plan.

DAY 348

Never allow anyone the opportunity to become comfortable in residing negatively in our lives; mentally, physically, socially or spiritually.

When we've fought through obstacles that many failed at, rose above valley lows that some perished in and escaped tragedies that still hold others captive; we're exceptional.

We're not the norm, not made from weak cloth nor see the same visions. We're capable of seeing past dark doors, eating the best in a desert and living in the overflow when there's oppression.

What someone says, believes or feels about us hold no weight to who we know we are. Be dynamic, a hard model to duplicate, a tough act to follow and someone that'll always be missed when we walk away.

DAY 349

People are talking, are we listening? Pay strong attention to what they're not saying.

Sometimes when asking a person how they are doing, we need to pause to listen for their answer. Pay attention to what's happening around us. There are signs everywhere, are we reading them?

There are signs displayed all around us to embrace, proceed with caution, retreat and/or engage with power. Know the signs. Our lack of observation could cost us so pay attention.

Expect the best, prepare for the worse but in either case be thankful.

DAY 350

Today we're going to start the process of evictions. Too long we've allowed people and things to overstep their boundaries, overstay their time and override our positions. Today, let's serve these unwanted guests their evictions.

Put these annoying enemies, leeches and pest out with the quickness. Serve them notice that they're no longer welcome in your mind, heart, body and lifestyle. They can no longer hold our finances hostages and in the red. They can no longer put us in sleep mode and relax on our hurt, discomforts and lies. They must be evicted and served with no extended leisure or time with us for any reason.

With this eviction, we're to include the No Trespass post and if violated, they'll or it will suffer not us. Let's be free today from the mind games, thieves, depression, stress, poverty, sickness, bondage and users. Serve and execute the eviction for immediate action, then swerve in the peace that'll cover us.

DAY 351

The peace that we can get you is far better than anything or peace you can get from someone else. There is a peace that is so deep that nothing and no one can disturb it unless we allow them to. This peace allows you to walk gracefully through hard situations, hostile people and attacks of the enemy. When we realize this, we will be stronger than ever. We do not need to worry about tomorrow's bills, health issues, how you're going to get through. We have no reason to worry, so today, let's stop worrying and start praying for that peace!

DAY 352

Whatever the fight, heartache or headache, remember that we can be your own healer. That heated discussion, big letdown, terrible news or undiagnosed report, we got know how and when to strut our accomplishments.

Inside discomfort can never be outside performances. I was asked over 35 years ago "Don't you ever have problems or bad days?" My reply was "yes, I'm human and have rough days and battles, I just choose to not exhibit them to people who would prey on them and be pleased with my struggles. I choose to straighten up my back, inhale, put on my best smile and take the world by storm. "When my hands hit my doorknob, "IT'S SHOWTIME".

I refuse to display my tears, hurts, fears or weakness to a people that care less and may be the cause of it.

No matter what's happening inside, when we step outside to this cruel and evil world, "IT'S SHOWTIME". Remain powerful, beautiful, strong and in control and demand. We own this because our Greater lives inside.

DAY 353

Life is truly choice driven and many of our choices have put us in chains. The good news is chains can be broken as we teach ourselves how to make better decisions.

Our choices should always include the effect it'll have on others, our future and the final outcome. Let's be so thankful that our bad decisions can be revised, changed or erased.

Today, as we look at our life, let's ask ourselves how our choices played a part in it and if not pleased then how we can learn from our mistakes so that we don't repeat it?

Remember INSANITY is doing the same thing over and

over yet expecting different results.

DAY 354

When we think about waiting, sometimes we feel helpless instead of helped. One of our weaknesses is waiting because we feel the urgency now. Yet, in our waiting we find that if we hadn't waited, we may have lost great blessings.

In the pains of our labor we need to be expecting something bigger than anything imaginable. Waiting for our doors to open, our request granted, our bodies healed, minds balanced and lives to change. Let's expect God to show up and out that those around us will be confounded, confused and conscious of the Boom in our wait. Don't hurry perfection, walk away from our destiny and limit our future. We're on the brink of an explosion that due only because we knew how to wait and expect.

We need the darkness in order for our light to shine and to be seen.

DAY 355

Whether we're feeling overwhelmed, near to a meltdown or unsure; believe that it's going to be okay.

Sometimes when hitting brick walls, fighting unseen enemies, tearing down lies and trying to figure out the next move; it's going to be okay. That door that just closed, the relationship that ended, the account that went in the red or friend that walked away, know that it's going to be okay.

Every storm must stop, every wave must inhale, and everybody gets tired at some point. We may not know when or where the point begins but we must rely on this; it's going to be okay.

Through our brokenness, tears, state of loss or change; remember it's going to be okay. Any day that we're combating a situation or listening to another person's plight; shake it off, wipe those tears, straighten up our backs and declare "It's Going to be Okay". Repeat as often as needed.

DAY 356

Never allow anyone to have that kind of power over us that they can master our life. Let's not let our enemies believe they can push buttons to get responses. Always make them think because we remain steps before them and own the footstool.

What they may be thinking, we've mastered and wrote books on. Let their plans be a whisper and vapor to the awesomeness and absolute truth.

Today, we can love some better from a distance and smile easier in just knowing that our truth is everything. Set goals, make strides, create opportunities and be boss.

DAY 357

We're awesome, and we're looking for a ridiculous blessing today. We're seeking to close some doors that's been purposely or accidentally opened. We also need to open the doors to our heart, finances, health, surroundings and future. We're waiting for things to turn around in our Favor. To open our spiritual eyes, ears and heart to be very sensitive to directions, people and plan. Yes, today is a great day and we lived to be counted in it.

DAY 358

All I could hear my spirit saying to me today is Trust the process. No matter what happens in life, who or what we lose, there's always a reason for it. Either it's to teach us a lesson or because it's in that person or thing's purpose to be gone. You don't have to lose something or someone physically; it could be an emotional loss, spiritual loss, financial loss, etc.

Often times we resort to "Why me? Why me?". But the question is "why not you?" We are not exempt from loss, heartache, pain, etc. We must remember what we are here and called to do and that's not to go on about what's wrong but to move forward and look at what's right! Death comes every day. It's inevitable-- so don't waste your time dwelling on what happened. Instead, focus on what tomorrow will bring.

DAY 359

If we want to know how much power we possess or our strength and patience; check out our test. Like any test, they come to try our attention to details, our training and our tools.

Everyone isn't equipped to go through the same test but whatever test we've been sent, it's a test we can win, learn and teach.

Most tests aren't easy or comfortable but they're able to pull out what's buried in us to overcome its failure. Some test brings us to tears, some to our knees and beds yet they all should bring us closer to our power source.

Within in us all is a power we many times don't tap into until we're tested but it's there always. Realize that we're stronger than we believe, better than we're perceived and possess more than what we've received.

The Kingdom is within us so, we're more than qualified

to overcome, disarm and take every challenge down with a smile.

As we breathe, so shall testing continue, know that we're tested on our skills, knowledge and tools so we got this.

DAY 360

We didn't lose our opportunity; we just lost our turn temporarily. Many times, we're rushing for our turn and yet not ready to be positioned. Everything and everyone have a position to play, some can even multitask. A clock is meant to tell time, not iron, or sweep the floor. When we play softball, we're given a position yet occasionally we're backing up another player (multitasking).

Remember, there is a time and season for everything. We may not enjoy the ride, like the position nor care for those attacking our lives BUT our time is set. Right in the middle of hell's fire, see the escaped assigned to us and know we're coming out. Fighting back tears, standing against adversity and swimming dangerous currents; know that we're not lost just better positioned.

DAY 361

When or what is the best way to make a request? Our request should be made known as needed or desired.

Making a request is far easier than having our request granted. Whatever we're requesting should somewhere line up with our heart's content, let's not doubt the outcome at any time.

We must have a plan for our request so that our purpose is plain. So, before making any request, let's make sure it's un-

derstood, considered and calculated on its delivery. I'm sure we've all been guilty of asking for something that later brought us heartache, disappointment and regrets yet we requested it.

When making a request, we must keep in mind of its ability to bring us blessings or curses. Think clearly before requesting and try not to make request under duress, temporary emotional highs or anger. Let's choose to make requests that will bring us and others joy, help and love.

DAY 362

Somebody is dealing with something that would blow our minds, if we knew. Whenever we're self-absorbed in ourselves, we'll never see others around us that need a 911.

It should always be our desire to be sensitive to those around us who are secretly fighting fearful battles. We're crying over a bill, a breakup, an emotional hurt and they're doing all they can to stay alive. Take a few days off from being #1 and listen outside for those that wish they could be in our shoes.

Think about every time we drink a half a bottle of water and leave it, now let's connect ourselves to those who don't have water, wells or see it as a luxury. Take time today and become more sensitive to others in our family, neighbourhood, country, and world that needs us to care, touch and help them; and do something.

DAY 363

Sometimes the hardest thing to do is show kindness and compassion to others when all you want to do is seek an eye for an eye. There will be people in our lives and strangers will come to destroy you and ruin your character. They will do everything they possibly can to hurt you. Even though you will feel attacked and burdened, do not let the flesh take over. It's one of the most difficult things to do but our reputation and sanity depends on it.

When you have someone/people constantly hating on you and seeking to destroy you, show them all of the love and kindness in your heart. That will kill them! Who knows? Maybe that person hasn't had the best childhood and has never felt loved. You could be the one to change that! So, let's have compassion for others and face opposition with kindness and a clear mind!

DAY 364

Today we want to be more intimate. Wouldn't it be wonderful if instead of masking, we would be unveiling when we meet someone?

Whether it's in the workplace, online or a date, if we were able to unveil and be transparent, things would be less complicated. Yet, there's so much time spent trying to peel back layers of hoopla before finding the true identity of a person.

Once the unveiling is available and the atmosphere is right, let's try to remove the mask so we're revealed for truth. Please don't allow this to confuse us into allowing anyone in our personal space that's undeserving. Only a selected few can treasure and embrace the revealing, so...

DAY 365

Always remember when our enemies are wasting time, we're buying it. Time belongs to us when we understand who and what we are, powerful beings.

We hold the past, present and future within us; that's time. Now, we must utilize our time wisely. We possess a spirit that knows all about time and if we're tuned in, imagine how powerful we can be.

Stop and think about how many bloopers we've made wasting time following wrong advice, directions and people. We say we should've followed our first mind (inner spirit).

Let's buy time, invest in what we desire to come not in useless, foolish and wandering things, people or places. Who's ready to buy time?

DAY 366

Respect can take us a long way in our lives. When anyone feels they've been disrespected, it causes friction in most situations.

We were taught to show respect to our elders and others and in return our lives were pretty fruitful. Today, the lack of respect is causing hurt feelings, anger and violence plus bullying. Respect begins within us then spreads outside of us.

Respect is mentioned from the garden to the relationships we're to have with one another. We don't have to like a person, yet we can still be respectful. Respecting another person's views even when we don't agree with them, is important in our walk. It may not be easy but it's always doable.

Honoring Aretha Franklin "RESPECT".

BONUS NUGGET

Do you know the top cause of death is heart disease? The thing about giving your heart away means you're signing up for something great but if you're not careful and continue to work out it can take you out.

Many of us have giving our hearts to people, places and things that have taught us how to be wiser with our giving. Hurt hurts and Love heals and covers.

Whatever heartbreak you're going through or have been through give it to the Universe, for when it has your heart, your treasure will be awesome as well. The Universe will take care of its own, it'll meet your expectations and go beyond your imagination, You may be a great help for someone, hold out your hands and see that you're a true blessing to those seeking you for help.

BONUS DAY

Even during our worse times, we must be confident that something great is going to be produced. We get excited when our life is in the uphill and mountain but become discouraged when it's at the down spiral.

Let's understand even when we're experiencing our lowest level, deepest pain, isolated areas, we're covered and adorned for a sweet comeback. We must know it's not always going to be easy; we won't always get a yes, things won't come together rapidly but, in the end, there will be a VICTORY.

It's sometimes when we're buried the deepest, felt the loneliest, been treated the worse is when we're being defined, approved and qualified for the greater. It's that last hurdle that we begin to doubt, the last penny when we think we're going

under and the final whistle that makes her hesitate but know that there's another in us.

This is just another win, another love, another move, another chance, another report, testimony and ridiculous blessing waiting to breakthrough. It's in the hard and bad times that we're pushed into better.

No one can fully appreciate a great thing, person or place until we've endured the bad one. Whatever the low is today; hold on, encourage yourself through tears and push because our best is still yet to come. Be like oil and rise to the top regardless of the pressure, so rise up!

www.ingramcontent.com/pod-product-compliance
Lightning Source LLC
LaVergne TN
LVHW010550160826
845677LV00013B/3067

* 9 7 9 8 8 8 9 9 2 4 3 2 6 *